Praise for *Self-Acceptance*

A real treat: Dr Barry's new book challenges the myths associated with self-esteem and focuses instead on achieving real self-acceptance. The reader is taken on a magical journey, from exploring why current ideas of self-esteem are unhelpful to how we can nurture ourselves and challenge our inner pathological critic and move towards true self-acceptance. This book is a joy to read, a real page turner, and incorporates all of the common sense, down-to-earth style that characterises the author. A very useful book for anyone affected by self-doubt and criticism.

Professor Catherine Harmer, Professor of Cognitive Neuroscience, University of Oxford

Harry Barry's critique of today's world, where we torture ourselves by comparing and grading ourselves against others, leads on to a humane and practical guide on how to shake off this habit and replace it with a self-acceptance of the utter uniqueness of the individual human life.

Professor Ian Robertson, Professor of Psychology, Trinity College Dublin, and author of Stress Test

This is the most remarkable book you'll read this year. Surprising, stimulating and guaranteed to change your behaviour. I found myself riveted by its compelling evidence.

Bruce Daisley, European Vice-President for Twitter, and author of the Sunday Times *No.1 bestseller* The Joy of Work

KING TOWNSHIP PUBL
NOBLETON BRAN

D0998950

Have we been brainwashed by the concept of self-esteem? Dr Barry thinks so, and in his latest book sets out to show how damaging boosting self-esteem can be to our mental health. Using real examples from the workplace, education and personal relationships, he shows us the healing power of self-acceptance. This book is different – it will challenge you and transform your thinking.

Dr Muiris Houston, Medical Journalist, The Irish Times, *and Adjunct Professor of Narrative Medicine, Trinity College Dublin*

Forget the battle for self-esteem. For good mental health, what we need is self-acceptance and Dr Barry's book does that brilliantly. Scrabbling for self-esteem doesn't work but self-acceptance – a deeper understanding of ourselves as people – is what can truly give us peace. Once again, with both case studies and analysis, Dr Barry shows us how we can reframe our thought processes to send the vicious inner voice out of our heads, and to accept who we truly are.

Cathy Kelly, bestselling author and UNICEF ambassador

Once again Dr Harry Barry has written a most helpful book. His chapter on the 'dark side' of self-esteem will strike a chord with many parents, teachers, employers and ordinary readers, and his chapters in the second part of the book on how to accept oneself (warts and all), take responsibility and try to change behaviours when things go wrong, offers a pathway to improvement for everybody in various aspects of daily living. This is practical as well as refreshing. *Self-Acceptance* will undoubtedly have some critics but the easy style and fresh approach to mental well-being, will ensure that this will be bestseller.

Professor Patricia Casey, Professor of Psychiatry,
University College Dublin

This book has the potential to transform the lives of people who read it and use it. It not only explores and explodes the myth of self-esteem and the damage it causes but it reveals the astonishing secret power of unconditional self-acceptance. It guides us through manageable steps in unconditional self-acceptance as the means to gently change our lives.

Sr Stanislaus Kennedy, social campaigner, author and founder of Focus Ireland and the Sanctuary Meditation Centre

Dr Barry's suggestion to us is to embark on a journey that entails a revolution! This is to leave behind the concept of 'self-esteem' and instead embrace and live a true form of 'self-acceptance'. After reading this book, I can only encourage readers to embark on this journey of self-inquiry to find out what is true for them: self-esteem or self-acceptance. As a mental health professional and as a private person, the answer is obvious to me.

Professor Bernhard Baune, Cato Chair and Head of Department of Psychiatry, University of Melbourne

Self-Acceptance is a wonderfully refreshing examination of the 'dark side' of society's obsession with self-esteem. Dr Harry Barry has put mental health and our understanding of it on a more solid footing by defining the myth around self-esteem and by asking us what we really mean by a term which is often banded around and held in great reverence by many. I hope it will be the start of many constructive debates around commonly used and mis-used mental health terminology.

Julia O'Hegarty, Consultant Senior Content Editor, Financial Times

Once again Dr Barry has provided a highly readable yet provocative book. By explaining the origins and current promotion of the 'self-esteem movement', demystifying it, and showing its deep and unhealthy flaws, he makes way for a healthy alternative: self-acceptance.

Professor Larry Culpepper, Professor of Family Medicine, Boston University School of Medicine

Happiness is a natural state we revert to when we stop doing things that take it from us. Through a misguided ideal, we have robbed generations of ever finding happiness by sending them off on a wild goose chase searching for a myth called self-esteem. Harry so brilliantly exposes this myth and leads the reader to understand the real path to happiness.

Enda Murphy, author of Five Steps to Happiness

I highly recommend *Self-Acceptance* to parents, educators and healthcare professionals responsible for the well-being of young people. This is an invaluable book, in that it questions the oft accepted truism that building a young person's self-esteem is important to their well-being. Drawing on the best scientific evidence he makes a convincing case that it has the contrary effect: increasing stress and anxiety. He especially makes a strong case for self-acceptance, it's an argument that I wish I had heard a long time ago, as a young parent and educator.

Professor Cathal Kelly, CEO, Royal College of Surgeons in Ireland

This is a book that challenges decades of a certain way of thinking and an ingrained set of beliefs. We live in a world where social media not only dominates our belief system but tries to destroy the concept of unconditional love. I just want to say, well done to Dr Harry Barry for your courage and trailblazing way in peeling back the very true essence of who we are and who we could be.

Senator Joan Freeman, founder of suicide-prevention charities,
Pieta House and Solace House

Through promoting self-acceptance as a means of improving mental health in every area of life, Dr Harry Barry's book succeeds both in offering a practical guide in how to do so and in raising awareness of this self-inflicted stress.

Dr Fiona O'Doherty, Clinical Psychologist

SELF-ACCEPTANCE

How to banish the self-esteem myth, accept
yourself unconditionally and revolutionise
your mental health

DR HARRY BARRY

I would like to dedicate this book to three very special children in my life – Ciaran, Sean and Saoirse. May they encounter a world of unconditional self-acceptance, free of the shackles of self-esteem!

First published in Great Britain in 2019 by Orion Spring
an imprint of The Orion Publishing Group Ltd
Carmelite House, 50 Victoria Embankment
London EC4Y 0DZ

An Hachette UK Company

3 5 7 9 10 8 6 4 2

Copyright © Dr Harry Barry, 2019

The moral right of Dr Harry Barry to be identified as the author of this work has been asserted in accordance with the Copyright, Designs and Patents Act of 1988.

All rights reserved. No part of this publication may be reproduced, stored in a retrieval system, or transmitted in any form or by any means, electronic, mechanical, photocopying, recording, or otherwise, without the prior permission of both the copyright owner and the above publisher of this book.

Every effort has been made to ensure that the information in the book is accurate. The information in this book may not be applicable in each individual case so it is advised that professional medical advice is obtained for specific health matters and before changing any medication or dosage. Neither the publisher nor author accepts any legal responsibility for any personal injury or other damage or loss arising from the use of the information in this book. In addition, if you are concerned about your diet or exercise regime and wish to change them, you should consult a health practitioner first.

A CIP catalogue record for this book is
available from the British Library.

ISBN (Trade paperback) 978 1 4091 8855 1
ISBN (eBook) 978 1 4091 8856 8

Typeset by Input Data Services Ltd, Somerset
Printed and bound by CPI Group (UK) Ltd, Croydon, CR0 4YY

MIX
Paper from responsible sources
FSC® C104740

www.orionbooks.co.uk

ORION
SPRING

CONTENTS

INTRODUCTION

How much are you 'really' worth as a person?

Just what is self-esteem?

Why is it a myth?

Is this myth damaging our mental health?

Why are our children in pain? Why are we not listening?

What is unconditional self-acceptance?

Why is it the secret to mental health?

These are the questions that this book sets out to answer. It is going to bring you on a journey of discovery; an odyssey that has the power to completely transform all our lives and the lives of our most precious assets – our children. It will hopefully open a badly needed discussion on the whole topic of self-esteem and self-rating and how both, in my opinion, are destroying the fabric of our society.

I fear especially for our young people as they become increasingly drawn into the world of technology and social media. The toxic cocktail of both, combined with an obsession with self-esteem and rating, is poisoning the lives of children and us adults, too. We owe it both to ourselves and them to honestly face up to the questions outlined above and, as a society, endeavour to answer them. Most of all, we need to enter and embrace the transformative world of unconditional self-acceptance, which we will be exploring later. How it can transform our relationships, workplaces, body image, schools and colleges and especially our mental health.

Self-acceptance is about more than just banishing the myth of self-esteem or challenging self-rating. It is about learning to be truly comfortable in our own skins while taking real responsibility for our behaviour. It challenges us to become mature, emotionally resilient human beings; teaching us to be both kind but also firm with ourselves. It is the very essence of good mental health.

It is also about who we are as a people. Where are we going? Do we truly value our mental health? Can we transform the lives of our children for the future? I truly believe we can. I hope you will join me on this journey of discovery.

Let's open our discussion by exploring the current understanding of how to best improve and safeguard our mental health.

After decades lagging in the wake of physical health, we are finally recognising the importance of looking after our mental health. To reduce the risks of anxiety, depression, toxic stress, eating disorders and, above all, self-harm and suicide, we must nourish this fragile component of our lives. It is like trying to protect and nurture a delicate plant in a hostile environment. It involves hard work and dedication, combined with a steely determination to grow a plant that will survive and mature even when exposed to adverse conditions.

But when asked how best to achieve this objective of positive mental health, most of us struggle to reply. The most common suggestions will usually involve making sensible changes to lifestyle and increasing our self-esteem. The first suggestion has much merit. Few can argue that working on diet, exercise, stress-reduction measures, meditation/mindfulness, sleep and reducing alcohol limits will not bear fruit.

Then there is the other strand to the suggestions: that we develop techniques to boost our self-esteem. Most assume that this is a sensible, scientifically and academically proven measure that will provide major benefits to our mental health. Tragically, as this book sets out to prove, nothing could be further from the truth. For this is a road that leads to nowhere. Even worse, a road that may damage our mental health, achieving the opposite effect of what it purports to do.

I can already hear the protests! Am I not flying in the face of every major academic and scientific institution that has for aeons embraced the importance of self-esteem?

But what if self-esteem was indeed a myth? A delusion? What if those respected bodies are basing their approaches on unsafe foundations? What if the concept of pursuing or boosting this myth or delusion of self-esteem is creating rather than solving mental-health difficulties?

Our children are our greatest treasure. Never has there been such an emphasis on the mental health and well-being of our children and adolescents. Never has this age group experienced such a level of mental-health challenges and difficulties. Suppose our obsession with self-esteem and how to boost it in this population was making them less emotionally resilient, increasing their risks of mental health difficulties?

Researching this subject led me to explore how, ever so subtly, the myth of self-esteem has inserted itself into many areas of modern life, specifically in areas such as education, the workplace, relationships and social media. How the self-esteem delusion is becoming increasingly embedded into our twenty-first-century culture, with potentially significant negative consequences, and how this myth must be exposed and challenged. For nothing has been allowed to get in the way of the self-esteem movement tsunami, which goes from strength to strength. A worrying aspect that we will also explore is the financial clout of the self-esteem industry, which has become big business, especially in the USA.

If one doubts their power, an article in the Cut online magazine of the *New York Times* (2018) titled 'How the Self-esteem Craze Took Over America – and why the hype was irresistible' reveals just how embedded the concept remains in American culture. It discusses the history of the movement, the many false claims made about self-esteem, how many of these have been debunked by academics and how boosting self-esteem has become a billion-dollar industry, with many 'vested interests' intent on keeping the concept alive and well. It appears as if there are 'big bucks' to be made in perpetuating the self-worth delusion!

A potent mixture of governments, academic and professional bodies, a powerful self-esteem movement, especially in the USA, and a multi-billion-dollar/pound self-esteem self-help industry, have all succeeded in convincing us of the necessity of expanding and boosting our self-esteem. Their core message: that boosting self-esteem is the answer to preventing most of our mental-health ills. Hopefully this book will trigger the beginning of a conversation that we in society need to have, and quickly, before further damage ensues.

I am aware that there will be many opposing voices to the main thrust of this book. Other voices have gone before me, that have also expressed their concern about our obsession with self-esteem and self-worth. Some of these I uncovered while writing this book; others I was already familiar with. We will be meeting many of them later. These dissenting voices – often eminent academics expressing their deep reservations on the subject – have had their views swept aside.

This book has been brewing in my mind for several years. I have been concerned for some time with how self-esteem has become a stumbling block in teaching us (especially our adolescents) how to cope with the harsh environment in which we exist. In *Emotional Resilience*, we explored many of the necessary skills to assist us in adapting and surviving the storms of life.

But everywhere I looked, when researching that book, self-esteem was put forward as the only real path to improving our mental health. My primary concern is therefore to demonstrate how our obsession with self-esteem is obstructing rather than assisting us in achieving this objective.

We will also be asking the question: if so much time, effort, research and resources have been put into understanding and improving the self-esteem of our citizens, why are our current child and adult mental-health services crumbling under the avalanche of an exponentially increasing workload? Could it be that we need to review again the world of self-esteem and the irrational beliefs underlying this mythical trait?

As a pragmatist, I have always argued the pointlessness of tearing down an institution or set of beliefs unless you can propose a decent alternative. And that is the real purpose of this book. I have worked for years with wonderful people seeking assistance with various mental-health difficulties. I would like to share with you a revolutionary new approach which has assisted many of them in transforming their mental health, with significant benefits for themselves and those they love. We will explore the origins of this approach, and how you, too, by learning how to apply it, can nurture and really grow your personal mental health. We will then demonstrate how this approach plays out in real life, through a series of clinical cases.

It is my hope that by the end of this book you will never think about self-esteem in the same way. You will become increasingly cynical and agnostic about its usage and the mixed, often confusing messages emanating from the 'experts' about what it means. It is also my wish that you will join those of us who have discovered another revolutionary path to nurturing and growing our mental health.

HOW DO I USE THIS BOOK?

The book is broken down into two parts. The first section explores why self-esteem is a myth, a delusion. It will challenge every aspect of this concept, demonstrating how it has been debunked by leading experts. We discuss myths that have grown up around it, the dark side of self-esteem and how much damage its pursuit is causing. It will also focus on the differences between self-esteem, self-rating and self-acceptance and the challenge facing us in how to introduce this self-acceptance into our everyday lives. The second section will explore the concept of unconditional self-acceptance and how to develop it and put it into practice in our lives. It will then explore – using clinical cases – how many people who were struggling with various issues relating to the workplace, relationships, education, body image and mental health learned to banish self-esteem and, through self-acceptance, to nurture and grow their mental health.

You may wish to go straight to part two for the more practical element. It is important, however, to understand why this obsession with self-esteem is causing so much potential damage, especially to our adolescents.

There is a wealth of academic and other references backing up the first part. This is important as there is a significant amount of solid academic information out there, challenging self-esteem and the myths associated with it, but a dearth of discussion about their contents. Hopefully this will base the premise that self-esteem is a myth in a solid academic framework, shedding light on areas that the self-esteem movement would prefer us to ignore. Those interested in following up on some of these references can do so by visiting the bibliography.

PART ONE

The Myth of Self-esteem

1. THE MYTH OF SELF-ESTEEM

What is a Myth?

A myth (which is derived from the Latin *mythus*, which in turn is derived from the Greek *muthos*) is best defined for our purposes by the *Oxford English Dictionary* as: 'a widely held but false belief or idea'. The implication of this definition is that an erroneous concept or belief about some aspect of our lives or existence begins to evolve and, over time, expands exponentially until it is finally accepted as a 'known truth' despite it being false. Someone proposes an idea or expresses a belief, sometimes containing a modicum of truth, which gradually begins to grow legs. As the concept is transferred, usually with some embellishments, from generation to generation, fewer people question the validity of the belief itself. Eventually it becomes accepted and absorbed into a culture and accepted as 'the truth'.

Part of the reason these myths persist is because we fail to put them through a rigorous scientific examination as to their accuracy. This often occurs because to challenge them in such a manner is unacceptable to the status quo.

All branches of science have experienced such beliefs or myths. Medicine, too, is littered with myths, some surviving for centuries before finally being debunked. The negative consequences for those at the receiving end of such myths were often serious and life-changing. Let's briefly explore some classical examples relating to physical and mental health.

Medical Myths – Physical Health

Bloodletting

The myth that physical illness could be treated by bloodletting abounded for centuries. It is terrifying to think how many people who were physically ill suffered and died from being weakened by the consequences of this barbaric treatment. In some cases, leeches were applied to assist in the process!

The bacteria hiding in plain sight

Peptic ulcers, affecting the stomach and duodenum, have been the subject of intensive investigation as to causation for over a hundred years. One myth which developed was that they were caused by an overproduction of acid in the stomach created by a mixture of stress, diet and family history. This led to some patients having parts of the stomach producing the acid removed, to reduce this hyperacidity. Meanwhile, a simple bacterium called *Helicobacter pylori*, regularly seen on slides from samples taken from the stomach of patients, was ignored as being of no relevance. It was eventually revealed to be the culprit. Nowadays, because this myth has been debunked, a simple one-week course of antibiotics and a four-week course of acid-suppression drugs can heal an ulcer, often for life.

Eating fatty foods is the main cause of coronary heart disease

Another common myth embedded in our modern world culture is that fatty foods, especially those containing cholesterol, dramatically increase our risk of developing coronary heart disease, leading to heart attacks. Our supermarkets have responded to this myth by providing us with shelves of 'low-fat' substitutes for normal healthy fatty foods. What is not so obvious is that if I reduce fats in foods, I must replace them with excessive amounts of sugar and salt to make them palatable. This in turn has in part triggered our current obesity and diabetes epidemic. These latter conditions have put us at greater risk for the future development of heart disease than anything to do with fatty foods.

Medical Myths – Mental Health

Lobotomy

The classic example was the barbaric practice of lobotomy, where the myth pertained that if one cut links between the emotional and logical brain, people would become less agitated if they were mentally ill. This had the effect of turning people into a vegetable state and destroying their lives permanently.

Depression is a chemical illness

The origins of this myth began with the introduction of the first drugs used to treat the symptoms of clinical depression. Because some antidepressant drugs acting on serotonin, for example, seemed to assist some people with this condition, the myth began that depression was therefore a 'chemical' illness. We apparently were lacking in key chemical neurotransmitters such as serotonin. The modern view of depression, however, is that it is not a chemical illness and that the theory behind this myth is completely flawed.

We now know from neuroimaging and other studies that the most critical finding in depression is a breakdown in the neurocircuitry between the emotional parts of the brain, which are overactive, and logical parts of the brain, some of which are underactive. This is combined with evidence of loss of brain tissue and increased activity in our stress and immune systems.

Suicide

Another common myth is the belief that asking someone who is feeling depressed about suicidal thoughts or ideas may put the idea into their minds and increase their chances of dying by suicide.

The reality is that it is usually a relief for someone to discuss such ideas and such a discussion may reduce the possibility of a potential suicide attempt. Sadly, this myth has cost lives and is one that needs to be soundly debunked.

The message is clear. Myths are not only misleading but can lead to unhealthy sequelae, some of which may be serious.

What is Self-esteem?

When investigating the definition, I discovered numerous, often diverse, explanations as to what it was, depending on which dictionary or source one used, contributing to the confusion surrounding this concept.

I have chosen the classical psychological definition of the term as it fits best with our common understanding of the concept in the fields of mental health and education.

In this scenario, self-esteem is defined as 'a person's sense of self-worth or value'. The term 'self' is self-explanatory! The term 'esteem' relates to the concept of 'measuring the value of something'. Under this definition of self-esteem, the measurement we make of ourselves is 'subjective' rather than 'objective'. This distinction is critical. Low self-esteem, based on the above definition of the term, relates to having a 'diminished sense of our worth or value' and high self-esteem as 'a heightened sense of our worth or value'.

One could argue, if some have low self-esteem and others high self-esteem, where does everyone else fall? Are we just average or slightly below average or slightly above average? Or maybe, as this book will argue, the whole concept is a myth or delusion to begin with. If this is correct, maybe we need to tear up the definition and indeed the whole construct of self-esteem and move to more constructive terms.

In psychology, there is also a perceived emotional attachment to the term self-esteem. This implies that my sense of self-worth or value can trigger relevant emotional responses. In this scenario, if my self-esteem is low, I may feel emotionally depressed, ashamed or anxious. This implied emotional attachment is important as, even though unexpressed, it is assumed to be present. But this can lead to significant confusion.

The Origins of Self-esteem

It is difficult to accurately pinpoint when and where 'self-esteem' began. There is a consensus that the term was probably first used by the great American psychologist and philosopher William James (1842–1910) in his work *The Principles of Psychology*. James is widely seen as the father of modern psychology, so self-esteem is one of the oldest ideas or concepts in this discipline. He believed that a person's sense of self-esteem could be determined as 'how successful or not they were in relation to areas of their lives, considered important to them'. This concept, as we discuss later, ran the risk of self-esteem being inherently unstable, completely dependent on our success or failure in such situations.

In the 1940s another famous American psychologist, Abraham Maslow (1898–1970), included the concept of self-esteem in his famous *Hierarchy of Needs* paper (Maslow, 1943) which described five important levels of needs that motivate human beings. These were physiological (basic needs), safety, love/belonging, esteem and self-actualisation. In Maslow's view, self-esteem related more to a need to be respected and valued by others. He believed that most humans have a basic need for stable self-esteem or self-respect. In his theory, people with low self-esteem sought attention and respect from others. Whereas those with high self-esteem sought respect from themselves. There are traces of Maslow's thinking in our current view of self-esteem, but overall his views have been superseded by modern definitions and understanding.

In the mid-1960s, sociologist Morris Rosenberg redefined self-esteem as 'a feeling of self-worth' or 'whether a person values, approves or likes themselves' and he developed the Rosenberg Self-esteem Scale (1965). This became a widely used measuring tool, even to this day, to assess self-esteem for research purposes in the social sciences.

But the modern 'self-esteem' movement as understood today began in the 1980s, in California, where State Assemblyman John Vasconcellos convinced the governor of the time to set up a task force on self-esteem. He believed that raising self-esteem would reduce crime, school underachievement, teenage pregnancy and alcohol and drug abuse. The task force came back in 1989 with a report (*The Social Importance of Self-esteem*) which simplistically blamed low self-esteem for most of the ills in society at the time.

The self-esteem movement had begun. As we will explore later, there was, however, little hard evidence to back up these extravagant claims.

There was a resulting special emphasis, backed up with resources, on boosting the self-esteem of schoolchildren. The assumption was that those with high self-esteem would succeed better academically and in many other areas of life.

The task force was disbanded in 1995, but the banner was taken up by a non-profit organisation called the National Association for Self-Esteem (NASE) whose aim was to improve the human condition by boosting self-esteem. Vasconcellos, who subsequently became a California state senator, passed away in 2014 but has left a legacy which lives on today in the USA and indeed worldwide. This has in part been consolidated by the self-esteem industry which in the USA alone is thought to be worth billions of dollars.

All based on the initial assumptions that all of society's ills were a consequence of individual low self-esteem.

But opposing voices in the UK and USA were appearing to challenge self-esteem. In 2001, Nicholas Emler (at the London School of Economics) in a major review questioned many aspects of the concept. By the early 2000s, the self-esteem movement in America had become extremely powerful. The American Psychological Association decided therefore to invite some leading experts to review all the literature available on the subject, to assess if many of the claims and assumptions being made were valid. The team, headed by Professor Roy Baumeister along with three eminent colleagues, first published their detailed findings in a major paper (2003). These findings were subsequently summarised and highlighted by them in another important piece published in *Scientific America* (2005). Overall, they questioned the definition, accuracy of measurements, proposed links between self-esteem and consequences and many major assumptions relating to self-esteem. They discovered that in most cases, the research literature did not back up the claims made. We will discuss their findings later in this chapter.

Self-esteem and its Importance

Mental health is seemingly based on having a healthy self-esteem. It is seen as a bulwark against anxiety, depression, stress, eating disorders and other conditions which threaten our mental health. It is also seen as something we must all work on, throughout our lives, if we wish to be content, happy and fulfilled.

Multiple research experiments have been carried out, to explore how concepts such as low self-esteem damage us in so many ways, especially our children. All claiming that boosting this magical but apparently extremely elusive state can have dramatic effects on our lives.

All the above assertions are based on the assumption that self-esteem:

1. Can be readily defined.
2. Is easily measurable (although completely subjective in nature).
3. Can be easily assessed as being normal, low or high (once again, subjective in nature).
4. Is easy to boost using appropriate techniques.
5. If low, will inevitably lead to significant problems and difficulties in one's life.
6. If high, will lead to a better quality of life, superior relationships and a general sense of happiness and well-being.

We will be examining later how deeply flawed many of these conclusions are. Yet due to the enduring nature of the self-esteem myth, they are stubbornly retained by all of us; academics, professionals and public alike.

Self-esteem through the Lifespan

The current understanding of self-esteem suggests that it is a stable entity but one that varies subtly throughout our lifespan. In childhood our self-esteem is assumed to be formed largely by interactions with parents and significant adults, whether negative or positive. Those children who feel listened to and validated will develop higher self-esteem and vice versa. If I am told that I am useless or worthless enough times, I will develop low self-esteem and vice versa. Children who are physically or sexually abused, or those coming from addictive or chaotic backgrounds, are felt to be more exposed to developing low self-esteem.

In adolescence, factors such as academic or sporting achievements as well as social interactions can also apparently affect our self-esteem positively or negatively. Self-esteem is assumed to increase in adolescence, and again in young adulthood and mid-life, before dipping slightly as we age. There is also a perception that our self-esteem, whether high, normal or low, remains reasonably stable throughout our lives and some even see this trait as part of our personalities.

The implication from the above is that self-esteem is something innate to us all, that can be measured, has a clear lifespan pattern, can be boosted with appropriate techniques and is critically important for our educational system and in the prevention and management of mental-health difficulties. But, as is so often the case in life, a concept which seems at first glance to be built on solid foundations turns out instead to be based on flawed information and beliefs.

This discussion on self-esteem is important for each of us individually, and for wider society. This unhealthy belief has led many of us to wander down dark and on occasions lonely roads, seeking something that, as we will now explore, is only a mirage. The revolutionary message of this book is that there is another path to follow. One that blows away many ideas pertaining to our current understanding of self-esteem, replacing it with a new, self-nurturing approach.

The Myth of Self-esteem

The concept of self-esteem is so strongly rooted in our Western culture, language, academia and understanding of mental health, that I as a professional have found myself over the years constantly using the term both as a doctor and an author. And yet, over the past five to ten years, I found myself becoming increasingly uncomfortable in using a term that I no longer believed was either accurate or useful. As a professional, deeply rooted in the Albert Ellis tradition (whose work we will be exploring later), I found the concept incompatible with the messages I was trying to impart to those who shared their mental-health difficulties with me.

But why is self-esteem a myth? Is it really 'a widely held but false idea or belief'? Let's explore further. We will be dividing our discussion of this myth into two parts.

1. The first will involve analysing and challenging the current definition of what self-esteem purports to be and exploring why this definition is flawed.
2. The second will involve challenging the unhelpful beliefs or assumptions that have grown up around the concept of self-esteem based on this definition.

We could call these beliefs or assumptions myths about a myth.

Challenging the Definition of Self-esteem

Is the definition of self-esteem flawed to begin with? Leading academics such as Baumeister have grappled with this question. Just what did the words mean in practice? On closer examination, I believe the definition is extremely flawed.

Self-esteem is defined from a psychological perspective as 'a person's sense of self-worth or value'. At first reading, this definition seems eminently sensible. It suggests we can put a value or worth on ourselves as human beings and that this value or worth is something that can be measured. In this scenario, it can be described as low, high or average. This measurement is of course completely subjective. The problem is that this definition falls at the first hurdle. What does the term 'self-worth' mean? Put down this book, take out a pen and paper and try to define just what it is. You will find yourself struggling. You will almost immediately find yourself focusing on the word 'worth'. What does this term mean?

Perhaps you might answer that it means 'how much a person or item can be valued at'. In this scenario, self-worth would then suggest 'the value the person places on themselves'. I could come back to you with the good-humoured comment: 'Will that be in sterling, dollars or euros?' Does this term not suggest that we are valuing the person as a commodity? Can human beings be valued or measured in this way? Is this false belief or delusion useful or indeed possible? To expand this discussion further, I am going to suggest that you perform the following exercise.

The rating exercise

1. On a sheet of paper, draw a straight line. At one end of the line write '1' and the other '100'. Now rate yourself as a human being between 1 and 100, with the former suggesting you are of 'little value' and the latter that you are 'right up there'.
2. Having marked in the score for your personal rating, now mark in where others would rate you.
3. Next, imagine you are called in to your manager's office and told your work was shoddy. Or word has gone around that you are a hopeless parent. With this information, where would you now rate yourself on the scale?
4. Then mark where you think others would rate you on hearing either of these two pieces of information.

How did you do?

The results of the first part of this exercise will impart some important information about yourself. Some of you will put your initial personal rating quite high, maybe 90 to 100. Others may mark themselves in much lower, possibly under 20. In practice, most of us will rate ourselves somewhere between these two extremes, often in the middle.

Reviewing your assessment of what others think of you can also be revealing. Some of us will once again mark ourselves at a lower or higher rating than our personal ratings. This will give some indication of the importance we assign to the personal valuation of us by others in our lives. We will be returning later to what these 'personal' and 'other' assessments tell us about ourselves.

Now for the results of the second part of this exercise. How many of you 'changed' your rating when asked about being incompetent at your job or being a hopeless parent? In practice, most people, if they are being honest, will mark themselves lower down on the rating scale. It is equally likely that your rating marking of what other people would think of you as a person, when these comments became known publicly, would also fall.

Did you fall into the trap?

This is an exercise I carry out regularly in small and large groups. In my experience, almost all of us fall into the trap and play the rating game. We immediately, almost unconsciously, begin to rate (measure/judge) ourselves as human beings. We are also quite adept at assuming that others can rate us in a similar manner. But most of all, we change our rating depending on the circumstances or situations presented to us during the exercise.

You might ask: why is this a trap? Is it not completely normal and sensible as human beings to rate ourselves in this manner? Or to allow others to rate us? But this is where we must think 'outside the box' and analyse why doing so is completely irrational and indeed damaging to us as human beings.

We must firstly ask on what grounds or using what scale did you apply these ratings? Is there anything in existence that we can use to do so? The answer of course is that no such scale exists. Because if it did, it should be a simple task to measure ourselves as human beings against other family members, friends, workmates or colleagues.

If I asked you, the next time you are sitting beside half a dozen of your friends, to rate them one against another as human beings, how would you fare? The reality is that you would struggle to do so. But why? The answer lies in the unique nature of every human being on the planet. There is no scale or book that can assist us to measure our 'worth' as a person or to compare our worth versus the worth of another. Yet based on the current definition of self-esteem, this is apparently what many of us believe we can do.

To really bring the concept home: imagine you are a parent and sitting around the table with your children. Suppose I asked you to rate each one of them in order of importance – that is, to measure the worth of each one of them against the other? Most parents would recoil in horror at such a task. Is not each one of them quite unique, with their own special little foibles and personalities? Where is the scale one could use to overcome this reality? There is no table to measure their worth. In your eyes, they are special and unique and will always remain so.

Why Are You as a Human Being So Unique?

Each of us as human beings are the product of the genes passed on to us from our parents and the environment into which we are born and in which we are subsequently reared. Although there are many similarities genetically between us, evolution has ingeniously designed that the DNA patterns contained in our genes and chromosomes, which come to us from each of our parents, are unique to us as individuals.

Think of each one of us as having a genetic fingerprint, like our hand fingerprints. We now know that every person's fingerprint is unique. So, too, is our genetic imprint. So even though human beings have similar physical characteristics, we vary significantly in cognitive ability, creativity, sporting prowess and countless other attributes.

What about identical twins? Surely, their genetic make-up must be the same. But studies have revealed minor changes between them, evident on more detailed analysis of their DNA. Identical twins who may be reading this book will agree that although they may look identical physically, each is different in so many ways from their sibling.

Environment also plays a major part in developing who we are as individual adult human beings. Where you arrive in the chronology of your family, for example, can play a significant part in how you end up thinking about yourself and behaving in the future. As can family situations, school interactions, friendships, relationships and so on.

The result of this magical interaction between your genes (many of which have been passed through countless generations) and the environment in which you are reared is the person you are today. The special, wonderfully unique human being who is reading this book. Thus it is impossible to measure one human being versus another. There is only one of you, even if you are an identical twin.

This might be the most important message in this book. You are a unique, special person and there will never again be another of you in existence in this world. You are a one-off. A rare and precious gift to those fortunate enough to know and love you. As such, you are unmeasurable and priceless.

Feelings of Worthlessness

One of the commonest manifestations of the self-esteem myth is where a person admits to 'feeling worthless'. The whole concept of defining ourselves as worthless is now firmly embedded in our language and culture. At first glance, it seems an accurate description of how a person 'feels' about themselves at a moment in time in their lives. Under our current understanding of the topic, they would be described as suffering from 'low self-esteem'.

The first difficulty is the word 'feeling'. A feeling relates to our emotional response to something. So, I might say 'I feel sad' or 'depressed' or 'I feel happy'. To say, however, that 'I feel worthless' is completely inaccurate. The more appropriate statement might be: 'I think (or believe) that I am worthless.' Our emotions are a response to how we think about something. In this scenario I might 'think' that I am worthless and this in turn might lead me to 'feel' the emotion of depression. To some, this difference might sound semantic. Are we just caught up in our use of language? But language is important. We need to be precise in the terms we use to describe our thinking and emotions.

The second part of the belief that 'I feel worthless' relates to the mythical idea that I can be assessed as worthless. We have already seen from our Rating Exercise and discussion on the uniqueness of the human being that the 'belief' that I can be rated as worthless is flawed.

Suppose you are, at this moment in time, in a bad space where you think or believe that you are worthless and as a result are feeling the emotion of depression. Try to define what a 'worthless' person is. Can you explain what it is about yourself versus friends or siblings or colleagues that makes you 'worth less' and them 'worth more'? Does this not suggest that you should be able to measure yourself against them as a human being? On what grounds? It is impossible to measure or even define what a human being is 'worth'. We are, as already discussed, much too special and individual to be described as such.

Self-worth is a delusion – a fixed, erroneous belief that we choose to believe is true. There will be some readers who, even after reading how impossible it is to define or measure the worth or value of a person, will choose to hang on to this delusion. Even when it is destroying their inner peace and mental well-being. The price we pay is the destruction of our mental health.

Diagnostic and Statistical Manual of Mental Disorders (DSM)

These ideas and statements in relation to self-worth and self-esteem have found their way into the most important diagnostic manual used worldwide to diagnose common mental health, the *Diagnostic and Statistical Manual of Mental Disorders (DSM)*. The current version, *DSM-5*, has taken many years and numerous international expert opinions to put together. One of the symptoms documented as part of the diagnostic criteria to make a diagnosis of Major Depressive Disorder (MDD) relates to 'feelings of worthlessness – nearly every day' (*DSM-5*, A7).

Whilst the intention is clearly to include a personal subjective sense of worthlessness, one must be bothered once again by the language used. We cannot 'feel worthless' but can only 'think or irrationally believe that we are worthless'. So, there is a mismatch here between what is a belief and what is an emotion. But it is the acceptance by this august body that a human being can be defined even subjectively as worthless that is of greater concern. Can anyone define just what the term 'worthlessness' means? Does it once again suggest that human beings can be measured or rated? That some can be 'worth less' and others 'worth more', as already discussed? It might have been more accurate to note that the person may 'irrationally believe that they can be rated or measured as having no worth as a person'. I am obviously expressing a 'personal' opinion here.

The other major diagnostic manual used by mental-health professionals, the International Classification of Disease (ICD 10) also uses the term 'worthlessness' as part of its diagnostic criteria for MDD. It is more specific: 'Self-esteem and self-confidence are almost always reduced and, even in the mild form, some ideas of guilt or worthlessness are often present.' (ICD 10, F32.) At least they use an 'idea or thought' of worthlessness rather than a feeling as in the DSM. But once again the term 'worthlessness' is used. Can anyone define just what this means? Again, the term 'self-esteem' is used, noting how it is almost always reduced in depression. All these terms are used as if they are definitive, scientifically proven and measurable. But are they? Perhaps we need either to come up with a definition of what the term 'worthless' means in practice, or else abandon and replace it with a more meaningful explanation.

Myths About the Myth

Now let's explore how a host of accepted norms or beliefs about self-esteem have emerged since the movement took hold in the 1980s, and how these beliefs fail to stand up to closer inspection. Despite this, many are still accepted as gospel by most of us, including professionals. Some of these 'myths about the myth' have strong roots indeed.

Why should we be interested in these myths? The answer is that many of these assumptions and resulting conclusions impact on our lives and those of our children.

These mythical assumptions include:

1. Self-esteem measurements are objective and completely accurate.
2. Self-esteem, especially high self-esteem, is critical to academic and occupational success, happiness, well-being, positive interpersonal relationships and mental health.
3. Boosting self-esteem is essential for the health and well-being of children and adolescents and reduces their risks of developing anxiety or depression.

4. Low self-esteem can lead to significant mental-health, educational and criminal-justice difficulties.

Let's challenge some of these assumptions.

Myth one: Self-esteem measurements are objective and completely accurate

We have already discussed how flawed the definition of self-esteem is. But it gets worse. It was decided that this vague concept could be measured and such measurements used in scientific studies. Several scales were then developed to measure self-esteem, with some widely used in research into the subject. The commonest and best known is the Rosenberg Self-esteem Scale (Rosenberg, 1965). This is a ten-item questionnaire in which the person answers questions about themselves and, based on their replies, gets a score of between 1 and 4 for each answer. Some examples might be that they are asked whether 'I certainly feel useless at times' or 'I feel that I am a person of worth, at least on an equal plane as others' or 'all in all, I am inclined to feel I am a failure'. One's self-esteem is rated depending on the score attained.

Is this an objective assessment? Of course not. It is a completely subjective, vague, unsatisfactory assessment of where I see myself as a person at the time of doing the test. We have already explored how difficult it is to measure the value or worth of a human being. Is this an accurate scale? No. If what it purports to measure is based on a very subjective assessment of myself, how accurate is it in practice? Yet this completely subjective assessment is used in many educational and psychological studies.

Baumeister *et al.* (2003) noted that such self-esteem scores are affected by people's natural tendency to make themselves look good. Most of us, when asked subjective questions about ourselves, tend to 'inflate' the answers to show ourselves in the best light. He also queried how accurate low self-esteem measurements really were, noting, for example, that those with 'low self-esteem scores' were also found to express negative views about many aspects of their lives. This makes sense, as if we have a gloomy outlook on everything, then such self-esteem scores are naturally going to be low. Can we truly trust a subjective negative self-esteem measurement of myself if I am negative about everything?

We can also ask: is this subjective measurement of your 'self-worth' easily influenced by what has happened to us on the day we are doing the test? Whilst the general assumption was that these scales measure our self-esteem over time, in practice, if asked about how one feels about oneself at this moment in time, most of us will notice that our self-esteem scores fluctuate widely (Crocker, 2013). But despite these reservations, variations of these subjective self-esteem scales remain the 'gold standard' for measuring how we as human beings assess our so-called self-worth.

The importance of objective measurements
I would like to return to the importance of objective measurements when doing research. My own experiences in working with an international group of experts tasked with putting together a screening tool to measure cognition in major depression has borne out the importance of having 'objective measurements' to balance out subjective ones.

Our group examined how our cognitive processes in depression, such as memory, attention, executive function (planning and decision-making) and psychomotor speed (how quickly our bodies obey our minds), were affected negatively in depression. The purpose of the group was to create an easy-to-use computerised instrument to screen people going through a bout of depression as to the state of their cognition. Some of their initial findings have been recently published (see Harrison, Barry *et al.*, 2018).

One observation noted by the group related to how subjective and objective measurements were so often completely out of kilter. One person, on being asked subjectively about their memory, for example, might describe it as poor, but this would not be borne out when assessed with neuropsychological assessments which are the genuine gold standard.

It is not that self-reported assessments made by the person are completely irrelevant. They do give an insight as to what the person subjectively believes to be the case. But we also require objective or confirmatory evidence to ascertain a more accurate or rounded assessment of the person's state – in this case, of cognition.

This distinction between subjective and objective is especially challenging when dealing with self-esteem. Since there is much confusion about the definition, and even more about how to measure it, either subjectively or objectively, it does seem as if findings based on such measurements may themselves be flawed. And that, as we will discover in the next two sections, turns out to be the case.

Myth two: Self-esteem leads to many positive or negative life outcomes

This myth underlies many of the false assumptions made about self-esteem. When the self-esteem movement began in the 1980s in America, it began to make several seemingly obvious and sensible connections between self-esteem and possible outcomes in our lives.

A typical example might be that 'if I have high self-esteem then I will be regarded as more likeable or better at relationships' and vice versa if I have low self-esteem. The implication being that it is the high or low self-esteem that is the *cause* of these consequences. So, if I am successful at something it is because I have high self-esteem and if I fail at something it is due to my low self-esteem. This suggested a strong causal link between both which does not stand up in practice.

Baumeister *et al.* (2003) strongly challenged this simplistic understanding, noting that it was not backed up by the research data. He commented, for example, that whilst many professionals, parents and others took it for granted that high self-esteem would inexorably lead to positive outcomes, this has not been shown in practice to be the case.

Huge claims were made by the self-esteem movement, based on this false reality. For example, they assumed that low self-esteem might be the cause of poor academic performance, rather than the possibility that it may have been the other way around. They also assumed that low self-esteem was the cause of crime, also shown to be incorrect.

This assumption of self-esteem as being causal, rather than being a consequence, has shown itself to be extremely flawed. A damaging myth we need to challenge. Otherwise we will be trying to boost the self-esteem of our children in academic situations, for example, on the assumption that this will lead to better outcomes. Let's explore this assumption in more detail.

Myth three: Self-esteem is critical for academic and occupational success

Academia
Let's examine firstly the links between success at school and self-esteem. This link was one of the major false assumptions made by

Vasconcellos, the politician who began the self-esteem movement in America in the late 1980s.

He argued that if they could improve the self-esteem of students, this would lead to significant improvements in their academic performances and future job prospects. Which in turn would boost the future economy through increased tax yields! The myth had begun and unfortunately has grown and developed as many legs as a caterpillar. It has now extended from just improving the school or academic performance of students to increasing their mental well-being and self-confidence, but more of that later.

To this day this belief still abounds, that if we can boost or increase the self-esteem of students, for example, their results will be transformed. Even though we cannot define or measure self-esteem and its so-called links to academic performance are tenuous indeed, the advice to all teachers and especially parents is to do just that! The link between low self-esteem and academic difficulties is often seen as an essential tenet of modern education. The implication being that parents must on every occasion boost the self-esteem of their school-going children or else they will struggle academically. The other assumption being that if they praise them incessantly, results will improve.

The expert findings

Baumeister *et al.* (2003) noted that whilst earlier research suggested a connection between self-esteem and academic success, modern research strongly disputed such links. When the data was reviewed in its totality, the assumption that self-esteem was the *cause* of either negative or positive outcomes in education was 'not supported'. Rather, other factors such as IQ and social class were of greater relevance.

They also commented that someone who is doing well academically may 'seem' to have a higher self-esteem, but this is not a causal link. More a consequence of feeling better about themselves because they are achieving better results. Of greater relevance, they noted that multiple studies pour cold water on the idea that boosting student's self-esteem will over time improve their academic performance. One of the core pillars of the original self-esteem movement was gone. Low self-esteem did not cause poorer academic performances and boosting self-esteem was ineffective at improving a student's overall results. High self-esteem was also not shown to be the main driver of academic achievement. Other factors were involved.

Other academic voices agreed. Crocker and Carnevale (2013) noted that in many situations people based their 'self-esteem' on their success or failure in specific domains and a classic example was academia. In this scenario, they based their self-worth on whether they succeeded or not in this area. It was not that their self-esteem was causing their academic scores to be higher or lower, rather it was the other way around. They were basing their self-worth on the results, which, as we will explore later, is equally damaging.

Crocker and Luhtanen (2003) had previously noted that students who based their self-esteem on their academic performances were more highly motivated to work harder. As they commented, though, basing your self-worth on whether you are successful or not academically is an extremely unwise thing to do. But it was their concerns about the dangers of basing one's self-esteem on achievements by trying to excuse or avoid failure that we should really focus on. They are sounding a warning bell for current school and college populations. In this scenario, students may focus more on how they can avoid failure or have appropriate excuses ready if they are not as successful as everyone – including themselves – expects. This is the origin of much of the procrastinating behaviour so prevalent in modern academia.

The workplace

It was not only academia that drew the attention of the self-esteem movement. Focus also turned to the world of work. The initial hypothesis of the self-esteem movement was that those with high self-esteem would be more successful in the workplace. This implied that those with low self-esteem would be less so, with the inevitable but false assumption that boosting the self-esteem of employees would lead to more positive outcomes for them and their employers.

But when Baumeister *et al.* reviewed the literature, their findings were like those found on academia. High self-esteem seemed at first glance to be linked to better performance, but there was no evidence that it was causal. This implied that if one was doing well at work, this would make one feel better about oneself.

Despite little evidence to prove that those with supposed high self-esteem will be more effective in the workplace, this myth still abounds today. The idea prevails that if I value my self-worth highly, it will encourage me to perform to a higher level.

The following quotation, often quoted in business circles and attributed to Sam Walton, the founder of Wal-Mart, sums this up: 'Outstanding leaders go out of the way to boost the self-esteem of their personnel. If people believe in themselves, it's amazing what they can accomplish. High expectations are the key to everything.' Whilst at first glance this seems to make sense, in practice the evidence is that boosting the self-esteem of workers has not been shown to significantly improve their performances at work.

One interesting finding by Baumeister's group was that those with high self-esteem seemed to be more persistent in the face of failure than those with low self-esteem. Whilst at first glance this seems like an admirable attribute, and in some cases it may be, they cautioned that this may not always be the case. For there are occasions when blind persistence in the absence of sensible reasons for continuing down a certain path may not be the healthiest behaviour to follow.

Leadership

But what about leadership itself? There is another misconception out there that those with high self-esteem make better leaders. A very relevant topic for the world at this present moment! This theory, which follows on from the self-esteem movement, assumes that those with high self-esteem are more optimistic, better leaders and will achieve better performances. However, these findings were challenged once again by Baumeister *et al.*, who quoted the results of a detailed research project carried out on military cadets by Chemers, Watson and May (2000), who found no evidence to back up these claims.

The myth that high or low self-esteem is critical to how successful or not we are, in academia or in the workplace, is still alive and well. Even though the basis for many of the assumptions made about the above statement are extremely flawed. It has also been shown that attempts to boost the self-esteem of either students or those in the workplace is ineffective and can be in some cases, as we will discuss later, damaging to the individual.

Myth four: Self-esteem is essential for happiness, positive interpersonal relationships and mental health

This myth has grown out of the belief that those with low self-esteem will struggle with interpersonal relationships and are more likely to suffer from mental-health difficulties such as depression. This implies of course that those with high self-esteem are more likely to be successful in interpersonal relationships and less likely to suffer from mental-health conditions. They are also assumed to be happier. But are these assumptions, which originated with the self-esteem movement and continue to this day, true? Let's explore the evidence.

Self-esteem and happiness

It does appear that those people with high self-esteem are happier in worldwide studies. But as Baumeister's group noted, how can we assess whether one is happy or not? Once again it is a self-assessment report. We have no objective way of measuring it. So, we have one subjective assessment – how do I value myself? – leading to another subjective assessment as to whether I am happy! Is it not more likely that instead of self-esteem making us happy, it is other areas in our lives where we may be successful or having positive experiences that are making us feel happy at that moment in time?

The reality is that happiness is an emotion, not a state! I have often argued that this search for 'happiness' in our modern world is like the search for El Dorado – a mythical city that does not exist. How much unhappiness is created by the belief that one 'should always be happy'. Another book beckons!

Interpersonal relationships

What about interpersonal relationships? Those with high self-esteem believe that they are more popular, have better inter-personal relationships and are less likely to suffer relationship breakdowns. Once again, the evidence uncovered by Baumeister and others suggests that many of these beliefs are false. When experiments were performed to assess what other people's views of the person in question were, the objective evidence did not support their subjective assessments. Although people with supposed low and high self-esteem managed their relationships differently, there was also little evidence that either had a significant advantage. Other than the hard-nosed observation that those with high self-esteem were more likely to break up relationships than those with low self-esteem.

Mental health

There is an embedded, almost delusional, belief out there that self-esteem is the best bulwark to protect our mental health. This was one of the founding principles of the self-esteem movement: the mythical assumption that low self-esteem led to a whole host of mental-health difficulties such as stress, depression, anxiety, eating disorders and even addiction. The solution was of course to boost the self-esteem of each one of us to prevent these conditions occurring! Once again, there is an assumption of causality here. The assumption being that my mental health is dependent on whether my self-esteem is low or high.

Let's explore the evidence as to whether this is borne out in practice.

1. Depression

The strongest perceived link has always between depression and self-esteem. The assumption is that those with low self-esteem are more prone to depression. Yet again symptoms of both are often based on subjective assessments. Those who classify themselves as having low self-esteem, as demonstrated by Baumeister, are also negative about many other facets of their lives. There are two schools of thought in relation to self-esteem and depression.

One regards low self-esteem as a direct cause of depression. The other regards low self-esteem as one of the consequences of this condition. It seems as if there is evidence for both, depending on whose research you are assessing. Once again, we must remind ourselves that self-esteem assessments carried out in depression are subjective and not objective. We know also that in depression our emotional brain has become completely negative, so we are viewing everything, ourselves included, through a dark veil.

Those people going through a bout of depression do tend on occasions to have ruminatory self-critical patterns of thought. They may be clinging on to irrational or delusional beliefs that they are indeed worthless. We will explore later where these thoughts and beliefs come from and how to manage them. But whether such ruminatory thoughts are enough to cause the illness is debatable. Many other factors and mechanisms are at play. There is evidence of significant changes in the neurocircuitry between logical and emotional parts of our brain, significant neurobiological changes, increased inflammation and activation of our immune system (see my other books *Depression* and *Flagging the Therapy*) and major cognitive difficulties which can be assessed by neuropsychological testing and metabolic changes. It is more likely that these are contributing to the ruminatory thought patterns noted above. Low self-esteem in practice has little to do with this condition.

It also seems as if those with high self-esteem, according to Baumeister *et al.*, seem less vulnerable to depression. This may be more associated with the fact that such individuals already have a more positive view of everything, including themselves, than those with low self-esteem. It is not high self-esteem that is protecting them from this condition, however. They simply do not have the underlying predisposition to develop this condition to begin with.

2. Anxiety

There are similar but weaker links claimed for anxiety. People with this condition are often assumed to suffer from low self-esteem. We are currently going through an anxiety epidemic amongst our children and adolescents. There is little evidence that 'boosting their self-esteem' is making the slightest difference to this crisis. There is, however, increasing evidence that smartphone usage may be of greater relevance than their 'self-esteem'.

We can also query whether those with low or high self-esteem cope better with stress. Initially the view was that those with low self-esteem coped badly and vice versa. Similarly to studies on other claims made in relation to self-esteem, however, there is apparently little evidence to back up these assumptions. The most that could be said is that those with high self-esteem seemed to recover better or bounce back quicker from setbacks in life. This may be because their emotions tend to be more positive or that they are less predisposed to anxiety or depression if stress does arise.

3. Eating disorders

What about the dark world of eating disorders, which include anorexia nervosa and bulimia? For decades, self-esteem was viewed by psychologists as a central plank in their understanding of both conditions. The assumption here was that low self-esteem was one of the principal causes. Some initial research suggested that low self-esteem could be a factor in bulimia but only when combined with a demand for extremely high personal standards (perfectionism) and believing that these standards have not been met in the form of being overweight.

With modern advances in neuroscience and psychology, our thinking about eating disorders has moved far beyond the simplistic view that these conditions are caused by low self-esteem issues. Eating disorders are instead more often linked with anxiety and depression, perfectionism, body image and a demand for control.

There is also a view that eating-disorder behaviours are like those experienced by addicts in general. We will discuss later the Pathological Critic and how this voice in our emotional mind is running the show in these disorders. Clearly this is a more complex disorder, with other significant facets apart from simple self-esteem issues being of greater import. This is not to say, once again, that how a person views themselves is irrelevant. It is important as it does give us some insight into their subjective assessments of themselves. It is more that there are other factors involved from a psychological and neurobiological perspective.

There are different models pertaining both to the underlying neurobiological changes in the brain seen in anorexia nervosa, for example, and the psychological concepts pertaining to the wider self and links with addiction (see Bibliography).

It is important to have this overview of eating disorders as being more complex and wide-reaching than previously thought. Otherwise the erroneous view, that poor self-esteem is the cause of these troubling conditions, might grow legs. Or the false delusion that boosting the self-esteem of our children and adolescents will reduce their incidence.

4. Addiction

Another powerful message which began with the self-esteem movement was that those with low self-esteem were more likely to become addicted to alcohol, drugs and smoking. The assumption was that those with high self-esteem were less likely to go down such roads. But when the literature on this was examined by Baumeister's group, no such connections could be made. There was simply no evidence that low self-esteem made us more likely to misuse or abuse alcohol or tobacco and only minimal evidence to back up connections with illicit drug use. Once again, other factors such as social background, family history of addiction, poverty, unemployment and personality play a much bigger role.

What Can We Learn?

The consequence of these false beliefs in relation to mental health has been a massive drive amongst parents and schools to find ways to boost the self-esteem of our children, adolescents and school and college students. In 2018 the *Key for School Leaders*, a national UK information site for school leaders, published an article on 'Boosting Pupil Self-esteem' with advice for teachers and parents as to how best to do just that. When an influential body such as this is supporting such moves, it demonstrates how embedded this delusional idea is in our consciousness.

Some school principals and teachers have expressed concern at how we are sheltering our school-going children, by constantly trying to build up and boost the student's elusive self-worth rather than assisting them to face the reality of life with all its difficulties. Never has there been such a drive to boost self-esteem. Yet never have they seen the level of mental-health difficulties experienced by students. Clearly there is a disconnect here.

The four myths detailed above constitute many of the false assumptions about self-esteem which have become firmly embedded in our twenty-first-century psyche. There are others, such as the false belief that low self-esteem leads to a greater incidence of anti-social behaviour. Once again, the evidence for this link is simply not there. Indeed, there is instead evidence that those with supposed higher self-esteem are more likely to become engaged in such behaviours.

Having now firmly debunked the myth of self-esteem and many of the myths that have grown up around it, let's now explore the alternative world of self-acceptance.

2. SELF-ACCEPTANCE

One of the challenges facing us if we banish the delusion or myth of self-esteem to the realm of bad ideas is how to replace it with a healthier alternative. Too often in life we tear down structures without putting in place healthier options. And so it is with self-esteem. We need a new, revolutionary approach. We are now going to explore a healthier, nurturing model of mental health that you can apply to your everyday life.

We must embark together on a journey, one where the ultimate destination is complete and unconditional self-acceptance. This journey can be life-changing for those choosing to embark upon it. We will explain where this concept came from, why it is so relevant to assist you in nurturing your mental health and, in subsequent chapters, how to achieve it. Finally, we will demonstrate how to put this concept into practice in your life, irrespective of the challenges you will face.

Let's begin by separating the terms 'self-esteem' and 'self-rating', for, as we will now demonstrate, there is a subtle but critical distinction between both.

From Self-esteem to Self-rating

Self-esteem, as we discussed in Chapter one, is defined as 'a person's sense of self-worth or value'. It is seen by most psychologists as a relatively fixed or stable trait.

Self-rating, on the other hand, is a much more dynamic, if irrational, belief or concept. It relates to any form of rating of ourselves. It seems at first glance to be identical to self-esteem or self-worth in that it also suggests that we can rate or measure or assess ourselves. It differs in subtle but critical areas.

1. Self-rating can be 'personal' in nature and most of us do tend to be critical of ourselves and rate or judge ourselves regularly and sometimes harshly. This personal rating once again relates to some vague assessment of oneself as a human being, which is why it is often confused with self-esteem. This personal rating is of course extremely unhealthy. Yet we all persistently play the rating game daily, throughout the whole lifespan. This is what you were doing when I asked you, as part of the Rating Exercise, to mark where you rated yourself between 1 and 100. The answer you gave was your 'personal' rating at that moment in time.

2. This personal rating is, however, quite dynamic in nature, and depending on what is happening to us at different times of the day or week can swing wildly from one end of the Rating Scale to the other. If any of you are active on social media, reflect on how your personal self-rating goes up and down like clockwork, depending on the online responses to the latest Instagram, Twitter, Facebook or other social-media platforms you are engaged with.

3. Self-rating, if personal, is however – often subconsciously – extremely 'conditional' on what is happening to us in our lives 'at that moment in time'. This, as we will be discussing later, was highlighted by the great psychotherapist Albert Ellis. Self-esteem is in comparison seen as a more fixed or stable entity.

4. Those who regularly personally self-rate themselves down on the Rating Scale, depending on what is happening to them in their lives at that moment, tend to be more prone to emotions such as depression and anxiety. Those at the high end of the scale in such situations are more likely to display emotions of frustration and tend be more perfectionist in nature.

5. Personal self-rating does not, however – if low – predict or lead to bouts of clinical depression. But when we are undergoing a bout of depression, as we will discuss later, we may find reasons to personally self-rate ourselves downwards, which perpetuates the negative thinking patterns underlying this condition. This distinction is critical.

6. The reality, of course, as demonstrated by the Rating Exercise, is that there is no scale or measurement in existence that can rate or measure a human being, so personal self-rating is also a false and equally unhealthy irrational belief or concept. We will be exploring this in greater detail later.

7. Self-rating can also be applied to our behaviour and skills. In this scenario it can often be quite healthy, challenging us to change these if required. This aspect of self-rating is essential to our discussion as it also marks it out as being quite different from self-esteem,

which is seen as more of a state and thus independent of behaviour.

8. The real difficulties arise when we merge our personal self-rating with our rating of behaviour or skills. In this scenario, we tend to personally rate ourselves up or down, depending on the success or failure of our behaviour or skills. This tendency lies at the heart of our modern adolescent mental-health epidemic! This was where William James started out from, in trying to describe what self-esteem was to begin with (the ratio of number of successes or failures in areas of relevance to us individually). What he was describing as self-esteem was in practice self-rating.

9. Unlike self-esteem, self-rating is not a goal that we achieve. Rather, it is a normal human tendency which can become extremely unhealthy if we overindulge in it. So, self-rating, whether personal or behavioural, is more the mechanism we use to assess different aspects of ourselves as human beings. Even if personal self-rating itself is a deeply flawed form of thinking.

10. A unique feature of self-rating is where we fall into the trap of allowing others to decide how we should rate ourselves. We call this 'other-rating' and it underlies shame and embarrassment. In this case, our personal assessment of ourselves is 'conditional' on what judgement or rating we believe others are passing on us.

11. In real life self-rating describes what we regularly do each day, more accurately than self-esteem, which is a much vaguer, nebulous concept. Self-rating is therefore more useful as a target for talk-therapy interventions.

12. We can regard the concept of self-rating as a

bridging point between the mythical, delusional world of self-esteem and our final goal, which is unconditional self-acceptance.

13. Unlike self-esteem, where we have developed several 'measuring tools' such as the Rosenberg scales already discussed, there are no such tools to measure personal self-rating. We have already discussed the subjective nature of the self-esteem scales and how dependent they are on personal observations rather than hard objective measurements. It is unsurprising, therefore, that one cannot come up with a personal self-rating tool. How can one measure or assess a human being to start with? And how could such a scale be accurate, if it existed at all, if my personal rating was completely conditional on what was going on in my life at that moment in time?

Why Self-rating?

One may justifiably inquire: why is it so important to shift the conversation away from self-esteem to self-rating? The answer is simple. Self-esteem has shown itself to be a less than useful concept, belief or idea when it comes to dealing with issues in our everyday lives. We do not go around daily, changing our self-esteem from moment to moment, depending on what is happening in our lives. Self-esteem is instead seen as a desired goal or 'state' we should be trying to achieve. I hope we have debunked this myth by now. But we do exist in a world where all of us are continuously challenging and 'rating' every part of ourselves and our very existence.

It is almost impossible to jump from the vague concept of

self-esteem to the deeper, life-changing concept of self-acceptance, as the former is so vague and out of touch with our everyday lives. Therefore self-rating, even if clearly flawed, is more valuable as a concept.

Of course, any form of personal self-rating is irrational, unhealthy and extremely conditional on what is occurring in our lives at that moment in time. But it does describe what we are doing in real life and is more open to challenging and restructuring. One may also inquire as to why we are so prone as human beings to play the rating game? Why has this human tendency to self-rate become such an issue in modern life? Why is it so threatening to the mental health of our adolescent and young adult population, both now and foreseeably for generations to come?

It is not easy to fully answer the first question. From the time human beings evolved, this tendency to rate oneself and others seems to have been the norm. It may have been an evolutionary relic, coming from the animal kingdom with its often-fixed hierarchical structures. One can understand the importance of rating one's attributes, skills or behaviours, but it is more difficult to explain the shift to a more personal self-rating. Clearly, our upbringing plays a major role in whether we learn to rate ourselves generally in a healthy, accepting manner or an unhealthier critical one. Irrespective of all of this, we can learn how to challenge and defeat this unhealthy pattern of thinking and behaviour.

It is easier to address the second question: why is self-rating such an issue in modern society? The answer almost certainly lies in a combination of social media/technology/smartphone usage and the way every single part of modern life is ruled by rating, measuring and analysing, which boxes us in as human beings.

Later, we will explore in detail the ravages social media is visiting on us all, especially our young people, even if some experts disagree with this statement. The false world of likes and dislikes, thumbs up or down, can lead to the most savage form of rating for those who are emotionally vulnerable whilst playing this ultimate cyber rating game! Unless we begin to prepare our children, adolescents and young adults to challenge the false news and beliefs emanating from this world, they will spend their lives playing the self-rating game. More on this later. We are all victims of the modern world's tendency to rate and measure everything. Science has been important in our lives and rightly challenges us to prove whether something is accurate or not by comparing and analysing data and rating its importance versus other information. Unfortunately, it has left us with the idea that 'everything' in life should be capable of measurement and rating. If we cannot measure it, then it either does not exist or we are doing something wrong in our calculations.

Business has absorbed the world of rating and measurement with open arms. It can use ratings as a stick to drive employees to either up their ratings in comparison to co-workers or else lose out on bonuses or risk losing their jobs. Unfortunately, some people begin to match their work ratings with their personal ratings and then start to suffer mental-health difficulties or significant stress as a result. It is a major issue for teachers, lecturers, managers, radio and TV personnel, not to mention the world of politics. All sink or swim dependent on the ratings.

Real life is not as clear cut and simple as a scientific research project. It is a messy, disorganised and chaotic place where most of us struggle daily to make sense of it all. When we introduce self-rating into the mix, especially personal self-rating, then matters can become complex indeed!

From Self-rating to Self-acceptance

If self-esteem is a damaging myth, self-worth a delusion and self-rating a useful but flawed concept, you may justifiably ask 'where do I go to from here?' or 'what am I left with?'. This brings us to the world of unconditional self-acceptance.

Before discussing this further, however, we must digress again and go back in time to discuss the groundbreaking ideas of an American psychologist, the father of Cognitive Behaviour Therapy, or CBT, and one of the greatest psychotherapists of all time, Albert Ellis (1913–2007). He was the first person to truly challenge the myth of self-esteem and attempt to replace it with healthier alternatives.

For the purposes of our discussion, Ellis was clearly uneasy with the whole concept of self-esteem and with the current vogue. In a seminal chapter in his book *Better, Deeper and More Enduring Brief Therapy* (1996), where he was laying out many of the principles of REBT for therapists, he noted that trying to increase the self-esteem of clients was fraught with pitfalls. One of his concerns was that the client would begin to believe that they only had worth if they carried out the suggestions the therapist made.

He suggests instead that the 'real solution to the problem of "self-esteem"' was to give their clients 'unconditional acceptance'. That they should learn to define themselves as 'good', just because they are 'alive and human' and learn to 'rate only the effectiveness of their behaviour, while not rating their self, their being or their essence'. (Ellis, 1996).

What a simple but life-transforming, revolutionary concept, which I would summarise as follows:

That we must learn to accept ourselves as the wonderfully special, unique human beings that each one of us is. Rather than being shackled by irrational myths or beliefs or delusions such as self-esteem, self-worth or personal self-rating, we are now ready to tackle the one part of our lives that we do have some control over and responsibility for – namely, our 'behaviour'.

It has long been my belief that these insights which Ellis shared with us over two decades ago have profound significance for us all. Note also how he makes a clear reference in the last sentence to the word 'rating'. It was Ellis's belief that human beings spent much of their lives either rating themselves or allowing themselves to be rated by others and becoming miserable in the process.

As the years have progressed and I have seen this concept revolutionise the lives of countless people struggling with their mental health, it is also clear to me that this approach is a more personally challenging and yet rewarding way to live our lives. At first glance it might seem as if we are letting ourselves off the hook in relation to many aspects of our lives. But on deeper inspection, as we will discover, nothing could be further from the truth.

Under the old flawed systems of self-esteem and self-rating, if I believed, for example, that I am a failure, then I can divest myself of any responsibility for my behaviour. I can sit in the corner and savage myself as being a complete failure as a human being. This of course means that I am not obliged to make any effort to improve myself or challenge why I have failed at a specific task and what I could learn for the future.

Ellis's picture of unconditional self-acceptance is infinitely more challenging. It suggests that we must learn to accept ourselves fully as human beings but agree to take full responsibility for our behaviour. This approach is going to lead to more fully rounded human beings, comfortable in our own skins but equally aware of and prepared to take responsibility for what we do. It has significant implications for many aspects of our lives.

Unconditional Self-acceptance versus Self-esteem

We can now see how damaging self-esteem can be in our lives in comparison to its life-enhancing alter ego, unconditional self-acceptance. Nowhere is this more relevant than in the realms of education and parenting. The current craze of trying to boost the self-esteem of our children has the potential to significantly damage their emotional resilience and prevent them becoming authentic, mature human beings.

Many teachers and principals are extremely concerned at this increasing focus on self-esteem. As one eloquently stated to me, 'Maybe it is time to cease trying to increase their self-esteem but focus instead on them improving or taking ownership or responsibility for their behaviour.' What they were describing was a radically different approach (steeped in the Ellis tradition) of encouraging young people to develop an unqualified acceptance of themselves as human beings allied to an increased awareness of their responsibilities in terms of their actions.

We are not teaching our young people unconditional self-acceptance, where failure would be understood by them as a natural occurrence. Where they could learn from their mistakes in terms of behaviours and skills, which in turn would allow them to grow and become more emotionally resilient.

But Ellis's message is not just for parents and young people, it is meant for each one of us. It has the potential to alter all our lives for the better. It could, apart from parenting and educational advantages, revolutionise mental health, strengthen interpersonal relationships, improve well-being in the workplace, increase our resilience to stress and most of all make our time on this planet a more rewarding, fulfilling experience. In a nutshell, we could achieve in one swoop what the self-esteem movement has failed to do over the past thirty years or so. What a revolution if all of us bought into this simple, clear but challenging message.

How can we achieve unconditional self-acceptance? How can you learn to shake off the shackles of self-esteem and self- and other rating? How can you become a warmer, kinder, empathetic human being, no longer afraid of challenging your behaviour head on when appropriate? How can you learn to put Ellis's amazing teachings into practice in your life? And most importantly, how can you learn to do so throughout your lifespan when the troubles of life come raining down? This is the task we have set for the rest of this book. How to make the revolutionary dream of Ellis come alive in your life! How can you truly nurture your mental health?

We will explore the challenges involved in achieving these goals unconditionally later. Firstly, let's explore the darker side of the self-esteem myth and its implications.

3. THE DARK SIDE OF SELF-ESTEEM

Why should we be concerned at all about self-esteem? Does it really matter whether the definition is vague and unsatisfactory? What difference does this make to our everyday lives? Are people not entitled to have these vague self-assessments about themselves? Self-esteem the delusion is not doing either the person or the wider community any harm.

Or is it? We are now going to take an in-depth look at the darker side of self-esteem. For what seems at first glance to be an innocuous, harmless concept is in practice best avoided.

The modern world has become increasingly complex. Social media in all its forms is insidiously taking over our lives. Family, community, political, economic and religious structures are coming under enormous pressure. Is self-esteem not more relevant amidst this maelstrom? Is it not even more critical in such circumstances to boost and increase the self-esteem of the individual and indeed the whole community? Alas, pursuing self-esteem as if something healthy and positive is adding to many of the difficulties, individuals, families and communities are experiencing. We are especially failing to see how damaging this pursuit is to our mental health.

In this brief overview, we will focus on parenting, education and sport, social media and mental health as examples of where the darker side of self-esteem is rearing its ugly head. We will also explore the potentially negative consequences that this obsession with increasing self-esteem can have for the individual, with a special emphasis on the rise in narcissism within our society.

The Self-esteem Myth and Modern Parenting

The modern nuclear family is smaller and increasingly more self-reliant than in former times, with pressure on both parents to work to support either mortgages or exorbitant rents. Couples are also having their children later, sometimes holding off till their late thirties or early forties. They are often far away from support systems such as siblings, parents or grandparents and small community back-up. The beautiful Irish concept that 'it takes a village to rear a child' has disappeared into the mists of time. One of the disadvantages of these social changes is the increasing focus on the individual child from the moment they enter the world. Each bundle of joy is a special and unique human being to be loved unconditionally. It is our role as a parent to nurture and take care of the physical and mental health of this child until they reach the age of eighteen and adulthood. Some parents are determined that their child will never experience the levels of discomfort they, the parent, may have experienced during childhood or early adult life. They will protect their child at all costs, from 'anything' that might cause them discomfort or difficulty, at any stage of their childhood or adolescence.

Other parents focus on 'self-esteem' from the beginning. They have been fed a diet of the importance of their child having high self-esteem. Nothing must damage this goal. The child and adolescent must be told how wonderful they are and sheltered from any possibility of failure as this might damage their self-esteem. Parents must step in immediately if their child is struggling with an issue or problem. If there is a difficulty at school with either schoolfriends or a teacher, it is the job of the parent to intervene to ensure that their child's self-worth is not impaired. As a parent you must also ensure that they do not experience any disappointments as this is detrimental to their self-esteem.

They must be allowed as adolescents to acquire the most expensive, latest technology because their peer group are being given the same. They must of course be gifted a smartphone at the very latest by nine to twelve, or the damage to their self-esteem by being left out of peer-group discussions may be catastrophic. Adolescents must be allowed to go to parties or concerts where parents know alcohol will be an issue, as to refuse might do irreparable damage to their self-esteem. It is also essential that children and adolescents are never denied money to buy 'essentials' such as the latest fashion or tech items or to go out. Even if the parents are struggling to keep themselves afloat financially. Otherwise they might think lesser of themselves as parents and damage their own self-esteem. Or even worse the self-worth of their children might be irreparably damaged.

Parents are genuinely doing their best to rear their children in one of the most challenging environments of the past hundred years. It is a hard job being a parent. There is no script, no perfect way. We do our best. But it becomes infinitely more difficult if we are burdened with the belief that everything we do for our children and adolescents must increase or, at the very least, not damage their self-esteem.

This concept is so engrained in our Western culture that we never question its authenticity. If we wish to improve the mental health and emotional resilience of our young people, we need to reflect on whether this concept is perhaps achieving the opposite effect.

Many of the actions described above, which seem at first glance to be sensible and constructive, may be unfortunately damaging the future resilience of our young people (see *Emotional Resilience*, 2017). We have a mental-health epidemic in play amongst our children and especially adolescents. The more we shelter and protect them, to boost and protect their self-esteem, the more anxious they will become. And the less resilient when exposed to the storms of life. If our aim is to boost the self-esteem of our children as a group, we have been quite successful. The same, sadly, cannot be said for their mental health.

A worrying trend in adolescence is the link in the eyes of parents between their child's self-esteem and subsequent risks of self-harm or suicide. Parents are terrified to say or do the wrong thing as they may damage their adolescent's self-esteem, which may lead to terrible consequences. This is a valid concern, as the incidence of self-harm is significant in our school-going population and the incidence of suicide in the UK and Ireland is higher than in other EU countries.

But is this self-harm epidemic due to low self-esteem? Is it that I as a parent am failing in my task and not boosting my child's self-worth? Or could it be that, in my desire to ensure that their self-esteem levels are high, I am removing natural resilience skills needed to develop and protect them from such risks?

It is no surprise that anxiety and fear of failure are some of the commonly quoted reasons why school children self-harm. The more we protect them, the more we refuse to expose them to the harsher realities of life, the greater these risks may become.

Parental Pitfalls

(a) Some parents link self-esteem and happiness. If you can boost your children's self-worth, then happiness beckons. Forget this concept of happiness. Rather, work on making your children more resilient and able to cope with the slings and arrows of life. Believing that boosting self-esteem will lead to long-term happiness is using one myth to strengthen another myth – neither being real.

(b) Other parents worry that if we do not 'give in' to the demands of adolescents, they may become depressed as their self-esteem will become damaged. The implication being that this in turn might lead to a self-harm or a suicide attempt. As discussed earlier, depression is a more complex issue in terms of causation. Increasing their resilience, rather than trying to boost their self-esteem, is more useful in reducing their chances of developing a bout of this condition.

(c) Others believe that the short cut to ensuring their young people will not suffer (in their words) from 'anxiety' is to boost their self-esteem. Constantly praising them, even if it is inappropriate. Constantly giving in to their demands. Never allowing them to experience discomfort or cope with the unfairness of life. Shelter them! Protect them! If I am successful as a parent in these objectives, I will ensure their self-esteem levels stay high and anxiety will disappear. Alas, this is also a myth and one we need to banish quickly from our minds.

(d) Another pitfall is to excessively praise your children or adolescents, with a view to boosting their self-esteem. A review of the negative effects of using praise in this manner was carried out by Brummelman, Crocker *et al.* (2016). They observed that modern parents in Western society tend to praise their children with a view to boosting their self-esteem. This was especially the case where the child was thought to suffer from low self-esteem. They felt that such praise was having the opposite effect, tending to lower their motivation and 'self-worth' when setbacks arose, such as failure. This in turn invited even more excessive inflated praise and a downward spiral. They called this phenomenon the Praise Paradox. So, as a parent, avoid this danger.

We need a new model for parents to adopt. One that challenges this myth that boosting a child's self-esteem is the short cut to happiness, fulfilment and reduced mental-health difficulties. We will propose such a model later.

The Self-esteem Myth, Modern Education and Sport

The original self-esteem movement believed that low self-esteem led to poorer education outcomes, and that those with high self-esteem would achieve better grades. The assumption being that boosting the self-esteem of students would improve the educational system and especially the academic achievements of the individual student. We have seen in Chapter one how researchers quickly put these ideas to bed. There is little to suggest that those with apparent high self-esteem do significantly better. The best that can be said is that this group may be more persistent. Most modern schools and colleges no longer believe that boosting self-esteem alone will improve educational outcomes, so focus more on boosting self-esteem to improve student mental health, as we will explore later.

Negative academic outcomes

But self-esteem is still lurking in the background and leading to some unexpected negative academic outcomes. Paradoxically it is with the high achievers, those who see themselves as being superior academically, that difficulties sometimes emerge. These occur when the young person either at school or college associates their self-esteem or 'self-worth' with being successful academically. This in turn can make them more anxious to succeed. Unfortunately, it can also lead to a paralysing fear of failure. They will then do everything possible to avoid failure occurring, aware that if this happens, they may begin to feel down. This can lead to either an excessive drive towards perfectionism, which exhausts them, or in some cases to procrastination to ensure one has a 'valid' reason to fail, or emerging with a variety of excuses if they do not achieve the high levels they believe they should attain.

I have regularly encountered this fear of failure and procrastination in young people heading for exams and in college. It is regularly accompanied by emotions of anxiety, frustration and on occasions depression. Occasionally if the young person develops significant anxiety with physical symptoms, they can develop secondary panic attacks and even phobias about attending school or college at all.

It can be significantly worsened if the young person comes from a high-achieving home background, where they feel pressure to perform well. Sometimes it can be related to siblings having previously been successful academically. Or parents either directly or subliminally pass down the message: 'We expect you to do well and will be disappointed if you don't!'

The origins of these difficulties can sometimes be traced back to the young person being informed from early on how 'smart' or 'intelligent' they are. They then assume that their worth or their value as a person lies in how successful (or not) they are at achieving the high standards they and those around them have come to expect. They have learned to measure themselves as human beings based on results, not effort! A classic consequence of the self-esteem delusion.

What can we learn?

It is essential as a parent to cease attempting to boost your children's self-esteem by informing them how great they are if they are successful in any area. This can backfire, especially if the child absorbs the message that it is 'they' as a person who are 'great' and not the work they have put into getting there.

It can also backfire where the young person has come to assume (as everyone has told them so) that it is 'them' who are smart or intelligent or creative. This can lead to a form of intellectual arrogance where they feel they should not have to work hard to achieve results. This can lead to procrastination and a belief that they should not have to try. If something does not work out, they will look for some scapegoat or excuse as to why this did not happen. Once again, it is the delusional belief that they as human beings can be measured in such a manner that is creating the difficulty. This can become a greater difficulty when the student enters college life without the balances and checks of school to protect them. This belief can lead to further mental-health issues if not challenged.

We must also be conscious that some children may not be as academically strong as their siblings. If they hear a sibling praised for their 'success' academically rather than for the 'effort put into getting there', they too may assign a value or worth to themselves based on their results. This can lead them to feeling anxious or depressed if not making the grade.

Schools, too, have a role to play in inadvertently feeding into this self-esteem myth. There can be too high an emphasis placed on academic results such as points or grades in exams. This can lead to both parents and teachers unconsciously feeding in to students the message that it is your 'results' that matter, 'not you the person'. Whilst most individual teachers will argue that their only wish is to produce a well-rounded, balanced human being, the overall ethos of the school may be sending out a different message. If students at school or college believe that their value or worth as a person is to be decided based solely on their academic results, they will struggle. Students, with the assistance of their teachers, need to develop new approaches to counteract this delusion and learn how best to deal with success and failure in their young lives. We will be meeting some students later in the book who encounter such issues and see how they learn to do just that.

Sport

Self-esteem and sport also regularly intertwine. Sport is a wonderful medium. It can assist us to learn some personal messages about life itself and the importance of team building. How sport involves hard work and effort, discipline and self-sacrifice. On some occasions it is about the individual, on others about the importance of the group. It is about the reality of winning and losing. Success and failure. How sometimes there will be great highs and on other occasions deep troughs. It is about the tears of joy and the tears of loss. Where the best individual or team does not always get the prize. Where the toss of a coin, the sudden shift in the wind, the faulty refereeing decision, the bounce of a ball, the badly timed injury can all influence the outcome. Like life, sport is not fair and never will be. It is a metaphor for life.

Difficulties arise, however, when we as individuals believe that our value or self-worth as a person is bound up with our success or failure on the field or at the sport in question. In this, it bears many similarities to the worlds of education and academia. Some children and adults are more naturally gifted from a sporting-prowess point of view than others. Whilst possibly struggling in academic or artistic worlds, they are comfortable in this domain. But if they are led to believe by parents or coaches that their only value lies in how successful or not they are at their sport, then trouble once again looms.

Some blessed with sporting skills may become increasingly anxious that they must not fail, and base their 'self-worth' on their success or failure. Others may become arrogant in a sporting sense, assuming that they do not have to make the same effort as others, yet expect to be part of the team. Others become depressed or frustrated if unable to reach the high expectations they and others have placed upon them. Others may drink or gamble to deal with these emotions. Some struggle with the unfairness of life if they are not achieving the success they expect. Those who are not blessed with sporting prowess can also fall into the trap of assuming that if they are not good enough to be on the team, then they are a failure as human beings, and become anxious or depressed.

At the heart of these issues once again lies the self-esteem myth and the delusion of self-worth being a genuine entity: that I as a person must and should base and measure my self-worth depending on my achievements in sport. This belief can be easily and unconsciously fostered by well-meaning parents who praise the young person from an early age as 'so talented'. This creates a double-edged sword. On one hand the young person begins to believe that it is 'they' who are talented and successful. On the other, that their value is going to be constantly reassessed, based on their continuing to be successful. Whilst some can handle this pressure, others struggle, and mental-health problems can emerge as a result.

What Can We Learn?

It is crucial that you, as a parent, cease trying to boost the ego and self-esteem of your children and focus more on praising the efforts they make in relation to sport. It also involves passing on some blunt messages about the reality of success and failure and the unfairness of life, and the importance of getting up and trying again. This is the secret to making them more resilient.

Coaches, too, must be aware of the risks of driving away some young people who do possess genuine sporting talents by focusing too much on results and less on looking after the mental well-being of those they train. This is best done by focusing on and praising the efforts being put in by individuals and teams rather than the results garnered. This can be a tricky balance to achieve as both the coach, the team and those supporting them want results, but it must not be at any price. Great coaches praise the efforts, focus on the process of how to achieve a goal and let the results take care of themselves.

Before leaving the subject, it is worth discussing how some parents and schools are so concerned about damaging the self-esteem of their children in areas such as sport that they insist that everyone who takes part in the event must get a prize or reward for just taking part. Whilst this is done with the best of intentions, to encourage young people to take part in such sporting occasions, there is a risk of sending out false messages about sport and more importantly life itself.

These false messages include:

1. Self-esteem or self-worth is so fragile that we must avoid anything that might endanger it and do everything in our power to enhance and boost it.
2. Life is fair, so to achieve anything of note, just turn up and be there!
3. There are no winners or losers in life. No matter how hard or not one tries, the result will be the same, everybody will win. The reality is that there will always be winners or losers in life, with the former usually being the person who has natural sporting or other skills and who has worked hard to improve them.
4. There is little point in improving their sporting talents by hard work and dedication, as their efforts will not be recognised or rewarded.
5. We only reward those who are, say, academically proficient and grade them accordingly, but choose to ignore those who have worked hard on their sporting skills. Are we sending out mixed messages as to what is important in life?

In both education and sporting spheres, our preoccupation with safeguarding and boosting the self-esteem, especially of young people, can lead to ongoing problems in the mental-health sphere. The key message for parents, teachers and coaches alike is to dismiss the concept of praising them when results are positive, which makes them assume that their value as a person is dependent on these. Replace this with a more sensible approach, where we laud the child or student or player for the efforts they are putting in. Add in a flavour of 'life not being fair' and 'the only failure in life is not getting back up again' and we will achieve our objective of preparing them for real life. It is this and not self-esteem that will assist them in achieving this objective.

The Self-esteem Myth and Adolescent Mental Health

What about mental health especially amongst adolescent populations? A core concept of the self-esteem movement was that boosting self-esteem would reduce incidence of anxiety, depression and addiction. With little evidence to support such claims, there remains, however, a mythical belief amongst parents, teachers and some professionals that self-esteem plays a major role in the causation of these conditions – with the implied false corollary that boosting self-esteem will make young people increasingly resilient to mental-health difficulties.

UK school principals are even today encouraged to boost the self-esteem of students, with parents strongly advised to do the same. In the past this would have been primarily seen as a means of boosting academic performance, but as this concept has waned, attention is turning to mental health, which is in a state of crisis, at school and college level.

The school mental-health crisis

Never has mental health needed such attention. If we look at the UK's Young Minds' Wise Up to Well-being in our Schools report (2017), the figures revealed are disturbing. They noted the following:

1. 90 per cent of school leaders had reported an increase in the number of students experiencing anxiety or stress, low mood or depression in the preceding five years.
2. A 44 per cent increase in referrals to Child and Adolescent Mental Health Services (CAMHS) between 2011 and 2015.
3. At least three children in every classroom had a mental-health problem. This figure increased to one in four if emotional distress was included.
4. One in twelve are self-harming, increasing to one in three girls aged fifteen.
5. Suicide was the most common cause of death in boys between five and nineteen and the second commonest for girls in the same age group.
6. The rates of depression and anxiety in teenage groups had increased by 70 per cent in past twenty-five years.

A UK Parent Zone report (2016) also revealed an increasing unhappiness in our young people, with 90 per cent of teachers believing that mental-health problems among their students were increasing and/or getting more severe; 62 per cent dealing with a pupil's mental-health problem at least once a month; and an additional 20 per cent doing so on a weekly or even daily basis. There has also been a worrying increase in the incidence of eating disorders. It is estimated that 1.6 million in the UK are affected by eating disorders. They usually begin in adolescence or young adulthood, but the age of onset has been reducing. Young males are now felt to make up at least 10–20 per cent of cases. We will be exploring links with social media later.

These mental-health statistics are being repeated in Ireland, the USA and many developed countries around the world. There has been an epidemic of anxiety (especially panic disorder) amongst school-going children in the past five years in Ireland, for example. The Mental Health of Young People in Ireland – a report by Canon *et al.* (2013) noted that approximately one in eight young adolescents had experienced an anxiety disorder, and by the age of twenty-four one in four had experienced either a mood or anxiety disorder. They also noted that 6.8 per cent of people will have experienced suicide ideation by age of thirteen and this will have increased to 19 per cent by age of twenty-four. The CASE study by Mc Mahon *et al.* (2014) showed that 8.9 per cent of girls between fifteen and seventeen were self-harming.

In the USA a similar pattern is emerging. The front cover of *Time* magazine in November 2016 was 'Anxiety, Depression and the Modern Adolescent'. It highlighted a superb article by journalist Susanna Schrobsdorff: 'Teen Depression and Anxiety: Why the Kids Are Not Alright', which unveiled a hidden epidemic in this age group. She noted that anxiety and depression in their adolescent population had been on the rise since 2012, often leading to self-harm. These conditions were present right across the social spectrum.

She noted figures from the Department of Health and Human Services that 2 million adolescents in 2015 had experienced depression affecting their daily function. She also noted that 30 per cent of girls and 20 per cent of boys, coming to a total of 6.3 million teens, were suffering from an anxiety disorder, according to the National Institute of Mental Health. And how experts feel that these figures represent the tip of the iceberg, as for example a 2015 report from the Child Mind Institute found that only 20 per cent of young people with an anxiety disorder ever receive treatment. As noted, it is difficult to get a completely accurate picture of the incidence of anxiety, depression and self-harm in this age group as it is so often secretive in nature.

In her article, Schrobsdorff attempted to delve underneath the surface to locate the origins of this mental-health storm. She noted, following multiple conversations with parents, teens, clinicians and school counsellors, that being a modern teenager was an exhausting, stressful, full-time occupation. Trying to cope with schoolwork, dealing with the world of social media, worrying about a future career and all the issues of the world today and coping with online fights and slights was exhausting them.

A similar picture is emerging in Ireland. It seems as if our adolescents are being overwhelmed, are less emotionally resilient and less capable of coping with adversity. Is our obsession with self-esteem playing a significant part in this maelstrom of mental-health difficulties – is it perhaps the hidden missing link?

Our focus on the mental health of young people is warranted, with 75 per cent of all mental-health difficulties occurring before the age of twenty-five. It is within this age group that the focus on boosting self-esteem has been greatest. Schools pride themselves on focusing in on the importance of self-esteem in their curriculum as a means towards improving the future mental health of their pupils. Parents follow likewise, hoping that persistent positive affirmation of the child and adolescent will lead to better mental-health outcomes.

Yet never have we seen such an avalanche of young people in crisis. Guidance counsellors and CAMHS teams in Ireland and the UK are increasingly stretched to deal with the stream of students in difficulties. More parents are seeking help for their adolescents struggling with many of the issues already outlined.

Numerous principals and teachers, as noted earlier, have expressed their concerns as to where this crisis is going to lead. They point to major issues such as anxiety in the form of panic attacks, school phobias, social anxiety, low-grade mood and increasing self-harm amongst their school-going population, and to a diminution in the resilience of many of their students. Their concern does not lie with the self-esteem of their students being low, but rather that this emphasis on self-esteem is making them less resilient and open to mental-health difficulties.

The college mental-health crisis

What about college life? There is often an assumption when young people reach eighteen that they are now 'adults' and prepared for the challenges of the real world. A significant number, however, will arrive at college, poorly equipped with the emotional resilience skills to assist them in coping with their new environment. Some may have suffered mental-health difficulties in school and carry them over into college life. Others are simply unable to cope with the changes associated with college life and develop fresh mental-health difficulties.

There is increasing evidence that the mental-health challenges faced by our modern school-going children are also present on our college campuses. A Center for Collegiate Mental Health (CCMH) Report from Penn State University (2015) shone a light into the darker side of college life in the USA. This report, which collected data on over 100,000 college students, noted a 30 per cent increase in counselling visits over the preceding six years, with a steady rise in self-reported distress from anxiety, depression and social anxiety.

Many of those seeking assistance had either attempted suicide or had engaged in self-harm. There had also been an increased incidence of suicide ideation during the same period. It was also reported in *Time* (2018) that in 2017 a report by the American

College Health Association indicated that nearly 40 per cent of a group of 63,000 students surveyed had felt so depressed that they struggled to function and that 61 per cent described overwhelming anxiety in the preceding year. The same article noted that campus counsellors themselves were suffering from 'battle fatigue' from coping with the tsunami of referrals for assistance.

A similar picture is emerging in the UK and Ireland. A YouGov Report of over 100,000 students in Britain (2016) noted that a quarter of students surveyed (27 per cent) admitted to having a mental-health problem of one type or another. Female and LGBT students were noted to have higher levels of mental-health problems than their male or heterosexual counterparts. Of those who were struggling, nearly half felt they had trouble completing some routine daily tasks. Depression and anxiety were the commonest conditions reported, with 77 per cent having depression-related and 74 per cent anxiety-related problems and a significant number suffering from both conditions. Eating disorders came in next, at 14 per cent.

Of great significance, over 60 per cent revealed levels of stress that interfered with their day-to-day lives and 77 per cent of all students surveyed revealed a fear of failure, with 20 per cent of these saying that this fear is very prevalent in their day-to-day life. Their primary causes of stress were study, finding a job after college, family concerns and relationship issues.

The *Guardian* (2017) noted that figures from the Higher Education Statistics Agency showed a significant increase in students dropping out of college due to mental-health difficulties. They also noted that there had been a 43 per cent increase over the three preceding years in those seeking assistance for anxiety and a 39 per cent increase for depression. Of greatest concern has been the doubling of student suicides over the age of eighteen between 2007 and 2014 and, as reported by the *Telegraph* (2018) based on data released by the Office for National Statistics (ONS), a rise in the suicide rate among UK students of 56 per cent in the ten years between 2007 and 2016. Also of concern was the information that female student suicides were higher than the traditional norm (one in three versus one in four).

Ireland, too, is in the throes of a similar college-student mental-health crisis. A Reach Out report exploring mental health in Irish colleges (2015) noted that the mental health of college students was much poorer than for the general population. They also noted how the My World Survey (2012) found that approximately one quarter of students reported mild to moderate depression or anxiety, with 14 per cent experiencing severe to very severe forms of both. And that over half of the sample of students reported suicide ideation, with one-fifth having engaged in deliberate self-harm. A more recent report (2018) on mental health amongst first-year undergraduate students reported that 59 per cent reported depressive symptoms and 28 per cent had suicide ideation. An *Irish Times* article, 'There is a tsunami of third-level students with mental health problems' (2018), laid out some of the current concerns. It noted that there had been a 40 per cent increase in requests for counselling in the past decade, with approximately 10,000 students attending counselling at any one time across Ireland, representing almost 6–8 per cent of students on every campus. They were seeking assistance with depression, anxiety, relationship problems and academic issues.

One feels that the figures quoted above are only the tip of the iceberg. Clearly, as in the USA, there is a brewing mental-health crisis engulfing the UK and Ireland student populations. Our young people are in pain and we are not listening.

The Role of Self-esteem in Our Current Adolescent Mental-health Crisis

Although these mental-health figures relating to our school-going and student population are a matter of deep concern, one can justifiably ask: where does the myth of self-esteem come into the picture? Why is it so relevant to this discussion? Is this crisis simply a response to a more difficult, challenging world where everything is uncertain and increasingly complex? Are these mental-health difficulties engulfing our young people throughout the developed world more related to a worrying trend of reduced emotional resilience, allied to the arrival of social media into their lives? In a nutshell, do many of our adolescents lack the critical skills to navigate the world they reside in? Whilst firmly believing this to be the case (which is why I wrote *Emotional Resilience*), I also believe that many have become trapped in the dark web of self-esteem.

This is because adolescents have been reared in a world where self-esteem is embedded into their psyche from the earliest moment of childhood. They have come to believe the myth that their 'worth' as a human being or person can be measured by themselves or compared to others. And that these comparisons are completely 'conditional' on how successful they are or not in different areas of their lives. Whether it be academic success at school or college, or on the sports field, in relationships or in their online world, their self-esteem depends on the achievement or not of these goals. This is making them increasingly anxious, stressed and prone to depression. It is also leading them into the world of self-harm and suicide, to cope with the distressing emotions encountered on failing to meet the goals set.

Is it not society perpetuating the myth that human beings can be measured as such that lies at the heart of the issue? Are we not keeping the self-worth delusion alive and kicking? We are the ones, not our young people, who need to start redefining just what it means to be a mentally healthy, non-rating human being, and pass this message on to our children who represent our future.

We are also assuming that if we boost their self-esteem at home, in school or at college, none of these mental health difficulties would occur. It is now obvious that the opposite occurs. The more we attempt to boost their self-esteem, the more we convince them that this is a goal worth pursuing. If they can boost their self-esteem, they will be happy and less likely to encounter mental-health difficulties! This approach is doomed to failure and may be leading to further mental-health difficulties.

Nobody is assisting them to separate who they are as human beings from what they achieve. Rather, by merging these two concepts in their minds, we are destroying their emotional resilience, making them vulnerable to the tsunami of mental-health difficulties detailed above.

Another false, unhealthy message fed to our young people is that self-esteem underlies their difficulties with anxiety or depression. If they are struggling with either, it is apparently because their self-esteem is low! We have already blown this causal connection out of the water, yet many students retain this false belief. This can prevent them learning how best to challenge both conditions.

There is a further subtle consequence of constantly trying to boost the self-esteem of our adolescents. It suggests that they are meant to be the 'greatest'. This implies that things should just naturally 'fall into their laps' and that hard work and perseverance are not required to achieve major goals in life. This can create difficulties for those who believe this myth, especially those who have found academic success easy to achieve prior to arriving at college. Suddenly 'real life' arrives and they begin to struggle. 'Life should not be like this!' For some, this can trigger anxiety, depression or substance abuse.

But as we all know, life is about hard work, discomfort and on occasions a little bit of luck thrown in. It is these attributes and not self-esteem that will help them achieve their objectives and nurture their mental health.

The Self-esteem Myth and Social Media/Smartphones

From the moment Mark Zuckerberg launched Facebook in 2004, the world was never going to be the same again. By September 2006, the website was open to everyone over the age of thirteen. Facebook was based on the concept that people would put up content about themselves and that others would then decide to like their input, or not. It was to prove to be one of the great success stories of our time. Zuckerberg had realised that if he could persuade people to compare themselves and their lives with others, then he was on to a winner. Facebook is now an international tech giant and its founder an extremely wealthy man.

Around the same time, Google and Twitter were also launched, the former in 1998 and the latter in 2006. It is difficult to believe how quickly these companies have grown to be the dominant forces in our lives, transforming how we communicate and think about ourselves. Information is the new currency and these companies have made fortunes in harvesting our personal data. They are controlling much of what we think, believe and do in our lives, often subconsciously.

At the same time as these three giant corporations were exponentially growing, a further technological revolution was brewing in the shape of the modern smartphone. This amazing device is the equivalent of a hand-held personal computer. Acting not only as a routine mobile phone, it also allows us instant access to the internet, emails, text messaging, sat nav, video games, a camera and videos, amongst multiple other functions. It is difficult to comprehend that the first modern version was only launched in 2000.

The perfect storm

What has now emerged is the perfect storm. A device we can carry with us every moment of the day, that is never asleep, that can entertain or stress us twenty-four hours a day as we so desire. A device built to encourage us into constant usage with its ergonomics and ease of design. A device designed to feed into the dopamine pleasure system of our brain through constant intermittent reinforcement. Add to this heady brew the world of social media driven by large social-media platforms such as Facebook and Twitter, where people are encouraged to share every personal moment of their lives with others. Add in newer platforms such as Instagram, a photo- and video-sharing social-networking service launched in 2010, and Snapchat, a multimedia messaging app launched in 2011, and we have the perfect ingredients for mental-health carnage. All designed to make us compare, compare and compare our lives versus the lives of others! Is this healthy for us as human beings?

Into this mess arrives self-esteem, the mythical belief that we can assign a value or 'worth' to ourselves as human beings. It is no surprise that this lethal mix of the smartphone and social media would awake with a vengeance the sleeping myth of self-esteem. The concept of 'like' or 'dislike' feeds beautifully into this learned human tendency to measure and compare ourselves. Over the past decade, this deadly cocktail of the smartphone, social media and self-esteem has invaded every part of our modern lives. All of us, both young and not so young, are living our lives through the eyes of these useful but infernal devices and online social-media platforms.

Of course, technology and social media have major benefits and add much to our lives. This is not a diatribe against them. I accept that both are here to stay and will become increasingly complex. They have enormous value. They are essential for connectivity, research, health, policing, business, marketing and education, amongst their many applications. The world has become a 'virtual global village'.

We need to reflect, however, on the secondary carnage created, especially for children and adolescents. We spent much of the previous section discussing the exponential increases in mental-health difficulties amongst our young people over the past decade. It is fascinating to match up the tech/social-media explosion which has taken place over this decade with this concomitant rise in mental-health problems. Both are running in parallel! I believe they meet in the dark world of self-esteem.

The role of self-esteem

All of us are easily drawn into the world of rating and comparisons. When we link how we think about ourselves with the results of such comparisons, trouble is looming. How many of us are taking part in a daily orgy of constant likes or dislikes on social-media platforms, flagellating ourselves if we are not winning? It is a recipe for dissatisfaction, restlessness and unhappiness. Not to mention the inordinate amount of time spent on these devices, with consequences for our physical and mental health in the form of diminished exercise, obesity and lack of sleep.

The results can be the ceasing of face-to-face communications between individuals, families, friends, colleagues, even strangers on the tube, bus or train. It may lead to a mother or father not spending enough face-to-face time with small babies and infants. Or couples or families in public areas such as restaurants all interacting with their devices and not with each other. How many of us are living lives with 'heads down', interacting with our devices, rather than 'heads up', interacting with each other? All in the pursuit of a mythical belief that my value as a human being should be based on the whims of others who are often equally aimlessly scrolling through their likes and dislikes! Or that my value or worth should be decided on whether the Instagram photo of myself is liked or not by others!

For large tech/social-media companies, self-esteem is a blessing in disguise. They don't need to persuade us that rating, judging or measuring ourselves as human beings is the best game in town. We are already there!

Never mind adults, what about the effects of this heady brew on our young people, especially our adolescent population? Already passing through that most difficult of phases, trying to understand themselves and their place in the world whilst detaching from their parents, they are also the group who have grown up during this technological and social-media explosion. To them, these devices and platforms are the medium of their time and they have embraced them with gusto. Quickly hoovering up the information required to access them from the earliest age, far outstripping their usually technologically impoverished parents.

They have come to demand smartphones as a right, and from increasingly younger ages. Parents have bought into this demand, with children as young as six to nine now in possession of these amazingly powerful machines. Whilst technically one should not be able to access sites such as Facebook, the reality is that many children under this age have such accounts. An Ofcom report on media usage and attitudes in the UK (2017), found 46 per cent of eleven-year-olds, 51 per cent of twelve-year-olds and 28 per cent of ten-year-olds now have a social-media profile. Of greater concern was the fact that 80 per cent of parents of children using Instagram and Snapchat were unaware of the legal age restriction of thirteen.

Why should we be concerned?

There is increasing concern about the use of smartphones and other technology amongst mental-health professionals, teachers, principals and some parents, and the impact that they, along with social-media sites and apps, are having on our children and adolescents. I have been highlighting my unease in the media, on air and at many public and parent-group meetings for the past five years. I spoke on the issue in May 2018 to the Joint Oireachtas Committee on the Future of Mental Health, expressing my concerns. I have been in favour of a National Protocol that would recommend parents holding off on providing these devices until the age of fourteen. One of the world's leading cyber psychologists, Dr Mary Aiken, who dealt with this issue in her superb book *The Cyber Effect*, is also in favour of delaying the age at which such devices should be presented to our children. At present, unfortunately, as mentioned above, they are being given to children as young as six to nine years of age. Dr Aiken, along with Senator Joan Freeman (founder of the suicide-prevention charity Pieta House and Chairperson of the Joint Committee on the Future of Mental Health) and others, were strongly in favour of the age of consent being delayed to sixteen in Ireland and this came to pass this year. This prevents the harvesting of information until that age. This is not dealing with the reality, however, that not only are children accessing these devices at inappropriate ages, but also social-media platforms that are developmentally unsuitable for them, with significant potential long-term consequences. This is the real-life situation on the ground.

But why should we concern ourselves about the current situation? There are multiple reasons, some of which I discussed in a previous book, co-written with a colleague, Enda Murphy, called *Flagging the Screenager*. They are also discussed by Professor Aiken in *The Cyber Effect*.

Take, for starters, the use of technology by small children. Many teachers are concerned about the lack of social and simple hand–eye skills of children arriving into primary education, and others about increased incidence of myopia due to use of iPads by children under seven. Or the concerns about increasing obesity levels due to the lack of physical exercise and sedentary lifestyle associated with their usage. And then there is sleep. Adolescents require over nine and a half hours' sleep and these devices are eating into these critical hours. The *Guardian* in 2017 reported on an Australian longitudinal study of 1,101 students between thirteen and sixteen found poor-quality sleep associated with late-night texting or calling was linked to a decline in mental health, such as depressed moods and declines in self-esteem and coping ability. There are also concerns about cyberbullying, excessive viewing of pornography, video gaming and gambling, increased risks of anxiety, depression and body image/eating disorders with usage of both the smartphone and social media in the adolescent period.

In 2017 the Royal Society for Public Health (RSPH) together with the Youth Health Movement published the results of a survey called #Status of Minds which examined the positive and negative effects of social media in a group of 1,500 young people aged between fifteen and twenty-four. They were asked to grade the five main social media platforms in relation to fourteen different aspects of health and well-being such as anxiety, depression, loneliness, emotional support, sleep, self-identity, body image, bullying and others such as FOMO (fear of missing out).

Even a cursory look at this list identifies many areas that are concerning parents, teachers and even young people themselves. Of interest, the young people graded the five most popular platforms in current use in order of least harm as:

1. YouTube
2. Twitter
3. Facebook
4. Snapchat
5. Instagram (deemed the most negative).

It is little surprise that Instagram should come in as the medium causing them greatest distress. Adolescents are obsessed with their emerging self-image. This explains the countless hours spent artificially tweaking pictures of themselves until the final product is sent into the ether! And for the rise in the infamous 'selfies', the hallmark of this current generation.

What lies beneath?

Underneath the adolescent mental-health difficulties created by these social-media sites lies the delusion that young people should and can base their self-worth or value on the positive or negative responses such as likes or dislikes received about the virtual identity they have created online for themselves. This has been described by Dr Mary Aiken as the 'cyber self'. Our adolescent population are increasingly living more in the world of the cyber self than in the real world, where life is significantly more complex and messier. This is resulting in a significant reduction in their emotional resilience.

If we delve a little deeper into the darker side of self-esteem and its interactive role in social media, more worrying trends are emerging. One of the most insidious is the tsunami of false messages social media is feeding into the emotional minds of our vulnerable adolescents. The modern obsession with the perfect body image or shape is an example. Difficulties arise when adolescent girls and young women link their value as a human being to the reactions that they receive to the Snapchat and Instagram pictures shared online. This is because they are linking image and the delusion of self-worth together – a lethal cocktail. This is strongly influenced by famous social-media bloggers and influencers.

Whilst the latter often live different offline lives from the online images they present, it is harder for our vulnerable young people to tease out the distinction between the two. Their cyber self becomes the barometer of how they think about themselves. If the barometer is up, all is well in their world and we say their self-esteem is up. If it is falling, their world caves in and we say their self-esteem is affected and has fallen. We have already explored how it is not their self-esteem which is rising or falling in such situations, but rather their self-rating.

Famous for being famous

Social media suggests that it is not hard-working sportsmen and women, or those who bravely and unselfishly risk life and limb for others, that we should admire most, but the opposite. 'Famous for being famous' is the new Holy Grail. It is not surprising that adolescent anxiety, stress and depression levels are soaring. If I base my assessment of myself as a human being depending on whether others feel that my online portfolio meets the grade or not, I am going to crash! It is also sending out another false message to them, that it is not hard work, commitment and self-sacrifice that leads to greatness. Rather, it is an ability to artificially manipulate my image or create the perfect online world that will decide if others think I am 'worthy' or a 'success'!

Whilst such approaches might work in the false world of 'cyber self-worth' it is of little assistance on encountering the real world. Here, failure is the norm, with greatness involving an ability to lift ourselves up repeatedly when life brings us crashing on to our knees. Here, love, empathy, caring for others and an understanding that life is neither fair or perfect are the skills that will guide us through the maelstroms of our future.

Opposing voices

Of course not everyone agrees that adolescents are being harmed by this obsessive usage of social media. An article published in the influential journal *Nature* (2018) by Professor Candice Odgers challenged this widely held view. She noted a decline in pregnancy, violence, alcohol abuse and smoking over the past twenty years as a counter-argument. What she did agree on was that those who are struggling in their offline activities or who came from low-income families were more likely to encounter difficulties.

Whilst admitting to the worsening figures in the USA of anxiety, depression and suicide in the adolescent population, she questioned the linkage in research studies between increased usage of social media and these figures. She noted that a large study by Przybylski and Weinstein (2017) in the UK found no association between mental well-being and moderate use of digital technology, and some small negative associations for people with high levels of engagement.

Whilst agreeing on the need for further academic research, the overwhelming feedback from schools, teachers, colleges, parents, family doctors and many psychotherapists, is that the combination of social media and technology is creating significant mental-health difficulties, with anxiety, body-image issues and self-harm seen as the most prevalent. Young people themselves are expressing concern regarding the pressures that social media is placing on them to be 'perfect' in so many ways and admitting to being constantly anxious if their online world is not seen by their peers as matching up.

Some schools that have banned smartphone usage have reported significant improvements in social interactions, general mental health and well-being. There is even early evidence of parents and schools coming together to ban or severely limit their usage, especially in early to mid-adolescence. There is, as already discussed, a clear, almost linear, pattern between increasing usage and growth of social-media platforms/smartphones and the rise in mental-health difficulties in our adolescent populations in the UK, USA and Ireland as well as the rest of the developed world. So, such initiatives are critical for the future.

If we could link such initiatives with a decision to bin the whole concept of self-esteem and replace it with a healthier alternative, many adolescent lives might be transformed from a mental-health perspective.

It is also interesting to note, as reported recently by Olivia Rutgard in the *Telegraph* (2018), how Silicon Valley parents, who have been at the forefront of the social-media revolution, are themselves limiting significantly the exposure of their own children to both smartphone and other devices and indeed social-media sites. Since these are closest to the origins of this revolution, this should set off alarm bells in the minds of all parents.

Will it be sociologists, however, rather than psychologists, who in twenty years' time will be casting a jaundiced eye on this current phenomenon, noting how we, as a society, allowed it to grow legs and spiral out of control. Perhaps they will be also highlighting the deadly links between technology/social media and the dark world of self-esteem and querying how we allowed the latter to fuel the former.

The Self-esteem Myth and the Rise in Narcissism

Before leaving the darker side of self-esteem, it would be remiss not to focus on its role in the rise in narcissism in our modern twenty-first century. This is timely, as our world stage is presently populated by leaders who regularly demonstrate classical signs and behaviours of this personality trait, who are equally adept at using social-media platforms to consolidate inflated views of themselves and their importance in the modern world.

The term 'narcissism' comes from Greek mythology. Narcissus was a self-obsessed, vain, handsome young man who wanders into a wood and comes across a pond. On stooping to drink from the pond, he comes across his reflected image and falls in love with himself as a result. As is often the case with Greek mythology, it doesn't end well, with the young man unable to leave the pond and his reflection, dying there in despair that the love he seeks is unattainable. Just think how poor old Narcissus would have got on nowadays in the world of 'selfies'! He would never have to leave the bedroom.

Narcissism is where a person has an inflated sense of their own importance, to the detriment of others. They require constant attention and live their lives seeking out the admiration of others. This personality trait is associated with reduced empathy for others, personal relationship difficulties, a tendency to ride roughshod over the feelings of others, an obsession with personal image physically and a delusional type of belief that they are better, smarter and more handsome than others. They hate to be challenged, and often become aggressive and unpredictable if this occurs. This trait is also associated with increased risks of anxiety, frustration, addiction and depression.

If many parents recognise some of these characteristics when coping with the typical modern mid-teen adolescent, they are correct. For adolescence is indeed a period of child development in which they are struggling to find themselves and develop a sense of self-identity, as described by Eriksen in his stages of human development. In general, they have worked their way through this phase by the time they are eighteen and this trait usually begins to diminish.

There is increasing concern, however, that this narcissist pattern is persisting longer into the young adult period. A seminal study of US college students carried out by Twenge and Foster (2010) demonstrated a significant rise in narcissism scores over a thirty-year period. Since then, there is a perception that this trend in college students has increased further.

But where does this trait come from? Brummelman *et al.* (2015) explored the two main theories. The first related to the child being exposed to a lack of parental warmth. The second came from social-learning theory, suggesting that children may grow up to be narcissistic if their parents overvalue them, seeing them as more special and entitled than other children. This would involve excessively praising them and assigning attributes of perfection, even if little evidence exists to support such claims. Brummelman concluded that the tendency to become a narcissistic adult was a result of the latter.

Once again, the dark side of self-esteem is appearing. If we excessively praise children with a view to boosting or hyper-inflating their self-esteem, it can backfire. There is an important message here for parents. We have already shown how trying to use praise to boost the self-esteem of those assumed to have low levels can backfire. Here we have the opposite. Parents may rightly throw up their hands in exasperation. What are we meant to do? One group is telling us to boost our children's self-esteem. The other is warning us against doing this. Whose advice do we follow? The answer is simple. We need to bury this myth, bin the self-esteem delusion and come up with a revolutionary new approach, which we will discuss in subsequent chapters.

There is significant concern worldwide about the appearance of major world leaders exhibiting the worst traits of this condition, who are adept at steamrolling through all acceptable human conventions. They are often, like Narcissus, infatuated with their own image at every level. It would be interesting to explore the backgrounds of such individuals to see the origins of such behaviour.

Apart from such leaders, we need to reduce the risks of creating such narcissistic individuals at family and community level by ceasing this obsession with boosting the self-esteem of children and young adults. Above all, we must cease over-praising children when inappropriate.

The rise of the 'selfie'

Before leaving this subject, it is worth mentioning the impact of technology and social media in the increase in narcissistic patterns in our society. Cyberpsychologist Mary Aiken is under no illusion that the increase in narcissism is interlinked with the dramatic rise in both over the past twenty years. In her book *The Cyber Effect* she notes that there has never been such an opportunity for all of us to share and show off personal information about every aspect of our lives. She especially focuses in on the new craze of the 'selfie' and the pressure on young people to focus on the perfect image for their online platforms, which we discussed earlier.

The risk, of course, is that this obsession with image can lead to the difficulties experienced by our young friend Narcissus, whereby we become totally focused on ourselves and less empathetic towards others. Where our cyber self is constantly at odds with our real lives. Where we may find ourselves inadvertently trampling over real people to get the perfect selfie. Dr Aiken gives several examples of this in practice. The most chilling relates to an incident in Los Angeles in 2014 where drivers were getting out of their cars to take individual and group selfies with a suicidal man hanging on to a bridge overpass. Clearly there was no empathy for the poor man in difficulties, more an obsession with getting a cool picture of themselves out there onto social-media platforms.

We may be heading into a perfect storm over the next decade. Our parents and schools are trying to increase the self-esteem of their children and students. The former in turn may be over-praising and reducing the emotional resilience of their children, increasing the risks of them becoming narcissistic in adult life. Meanwhile we are giving them smartphones at increasingly earlier ages and turning a blind eye to the age at which they join social-media platforms. They are then exposed to a narcissistic culture online where it is often all about 'me' and my perfect image and life, and less about others and their well-being. Once again, the potential darker side of self-esteem may become exposed.

4. THE CHALLENGE

We have discussed in detail how self-esteem, assumed by many of us to be an essential part of who we are, is, in practice, a delusion, a myth, a mirage. Something indefinable, always there in the distance but depressingly out of our reach! How many of the myths that have developed concerning self-esteem have also been shown to be false. And how this delusion or myth has a dark side. We also explored the importance of self-acceptance and that only unconditional self-acceptance can allow us to become truly free and comfortable with ourselves whilst accepting responsibility for our behaviour.

'But what about real life?' I can hear you say. Is life not extremely complex and full of pain, suffering and practical difficulties apart from all the wonderful joys of being alive as a human being? Do we all not exist in different domains such as work, relationships, academia and so on? Do we not struggle to cope with issues such as parenting, mental illness and body image, amongst others? How can we apply these concepts, however acceptable in theory, to the often-bleak landscapes of life that many find themselves inhabiting? Is banishing concepts such as self-esteem to the wilderness and challenging personal ratings really going to make any significant difference to 'your' life?

How, in practice, can you banish vague notions of self-esteem and replace them with something real and tangible? Words and concepts are important, but what really matters are the everyday details of our busy lives.

How do you, as a person, learn how to achieve this intangible goal of unconditional self-acceptance or how to put it into practice in your life? How can you, at whatever stage of life that you are in, or whatever situation or domain you find yourself dwelling in, learn to apply such noble concepts in practice? Is this not the challenge for us all? How do we integrate these ideas into our busy lives? How do we make unconditional self-acceptance meaningful when the cold, harsh winds of life are blowing?

In the second part of this book, I am going to try to honestly face this challenge. In the next chapter, we will show you how to develop and grow unconditional self-acceptance. In subsequent chapters, using clinical cases, we will see how this works out in practice.

I think every person will see himself or herself in the stories of those we are about to meet. People who have learned the wisdom of banishing self-esteem and self-rating and embraced instead the joy of true unconditional self-acceptance. Who have learned how to truly nurture and grow their mental health. We will take five key areas of modern everyday life and show in each case how to move from the mythical belief of self-esteem to developing unconditional self-acceptance. These five areas, which feed relentlessly into the world of rating, include the following:

1. Education
2. Personal relationships

3. The workplace
4. Body image
5. Mental health.

In the first part of the book, we reviewed much of the research and data out there relating to some of these areas and their connections to the worlds of self-esteem and self-rating. This was important as it bases our discussion in a solid foundation of scientific and academic information. It allows us to detach from the pyrite the foundations of self-esteem and move to the solid base of self-acceptance. It also frees us up to discuss what is the real objective of this book: understanding emotionally how unconditional self-acceptance can transform your life.

The second part of this book will be more about the personal stories and less about the 'research'. I hope you will accompany me on this journey of discovery. If you can learn to integrate many of the concepts discussed into your own life, the mental-health rewards garnered will be rich indeed.

With us on our journey will be Dr Jim, whom we met in previous books, a GP using CBT principles to assist us in achieving our goals. As we will be using CBT concepts for the duration of the book, let's briefly divert to explain what this is before advancing further.

Cognitive Behaviour Therapy

Cognitive Behaviour Therapy or CBT is based on two simple but profound concepts: first, that our thoughts influence our emotions, which influence behaviour, so what we think affects what we feel and do; and second, that it is not what happens to us in life that matters, but how we choose to interpret it. These form the basis of all therapy disciplines within CBT. I have discussed this form of therapy in detail in previous books and will only touch briefly on it here, with an emphasis on Ellis.

Ellis, whom we met earlier, is regarded as the father of CBT. Ellis's genius was to highlight what had been known for thousands of years: 'It is not what happens to us in life that upsets us and causes us so much grief, but rather how we interpret it.' He believed, as discussed earlier, that the latter was based on simple inbuilt belief systems that we develop as human beings mainly due to our experiences when growing up and developing. He called them Rational and Irrational Beliefs.

Ellis developed a simple ABC model:

A

'A' stands for 'activating event'. This is an event that sets up a certain chain of thoughts, emotions and behaviours. It can refer to an external event – either present or future – or an internal one, such as a memory, mental image, thought or dream. A useful way of examining the activating event is to divide it into the 'trigger', the actual event that starts the ball rolling, and the 'inference' we assign to that trigger – how we view the event. In some cases – involving anxiety, for example – this involves assigning a danger to the triggering event.

B

'B' stands for 'belief', an all-encompassing term which includes: our thoughts; our demands on ourselves, the world and others; our attitudes; and the meaning we attach to internal and external events in our lives. It is through our beliefs that we assess and interpret triggers. These beliefs can be rational or irrational.

C

'C' stands for 'consequences', an all-inclusive term which can include emotional and physical experiences, and especially the behavioural responses that result from A and B.

What this model does is allow us to explore why we become anxious or frustrated or depressed or ashamed, for example, when something negative occurs in our lives. It assists us in teasing out why it is bothering us, what irrational beliefs are being triggered and what unhealthy behaviours are adopted by us to deal with the negative emotions which flow from such beliefs.

We will see in the many cases that follow how useful this model can be in assisting us to change our negative thinking patterns and behaviours.

Dr Jim will be using the ABC model in assisting these patients to banish concepts of self-esteem, challenge self-/other-rating and to develop what Ellis saw as the real secret to good mental health – unconditional self-acceptance. The cases are explored and discussed exactly as would happen if you were personally engaging with Dr Jim, to make them increasingly meaningful for you.

PART TWO

Unconditional Self-acceptance

5. THE PATHOLOGICAL CRITIC

In Chapter two, we discussed how human beings have a built-in propensity to self-rate. It is important to meet the culprit creating much of the irrational thinking patterns behind this tendency to self-flagellate. We call it the 'Pathological Critic'.

The Pathological Critic

The term Pathological Critic was coined by the psychologist Eugene Sagan to describe the negative inner critical voice we all possess. We encounter this nasty individual regularly throughout our busy everyday lives. Sometimes his voice is male, on other occasions female. His or her voice emanates from the deeper recesses of our emotional mind. This is the inner voice which drags us down and constantly nags and criticises us at every available opportunity. 'You are just not good enough', 'You are useless at coping', 'You are so stupid', 'You are ugly', 'You are never going to amount to anything'.

The PC is expert at finding our weaknesses or areas of our lives where we struggle. It could be our appearance, social skills, job performances, sporting prowess, academic achievements or relationships. It will always find our vulnerable spot and stick the knife in!

The critic is created by the many and varied experiences we have in our childhood, adolescence and young adult life, especially the first two. Children are like sponges who absorb positive and negative messages from their environment. Our developing brain does seem to be hardwired to focus more on the negative (although the good news is that this reverses in mid-life, where our brain focuses more on the positive). So, any form of criticism or negative comparison with others becomes quickly entrenched in our emotional memory banks. As we emerge into adulthood, these memories tend to bubble up any time we encounter negative situations in our lives.

Most of the time our rational brain can keep some check on the critic, although we are all aware of occasions where it gets out of control and we lacerate ourselves internally in our emotional mind, when mistakes are made, or failures occur. In situations when the critic does get significantly out of control, it can lead to us experiencing unhealthy negative emotions such as anxiety, depression, shame or guilt. We can all relate to these occasions, some more than others. But generally, we can keep the PC under our thumb.

Once again there has been a mythical belief that self-esteem can be linked to how much the critic is running one's life. The suggestion being that if my parents, for example, were too critical of me as a child, my inner critic will become extremely negative and 'damage' my self-esteem. This leads naturally to the belief that over-praising my child should reverse the process. There is also a tendency to assume that if I have an overactive PC, I will automatically tend to have low self-esteem. We have already debunked many of these beliefs.

The PC is also felt to underlie the 'impostor syndrome' which so many of us experience from time to time, especially those who find themselves in positions of responsibility or in the public eye. This is quite a common experience and there will be many of you who can relate to it. It refers to the belief emanating from our emotional mind that we are frauds, putting on an appearance outwardly of competence and self-belief while internally we are consumed by doubts and anxiety that people will eventually see through us as the impostors our PC is trying to make us feel. Many highly successful women have revealed publicly how they struggle with this belief and how it can undermine their confidence.

But what happens when the voice of the PC within our emotional brain becomes a dominant force? Where the capacity of the rational mind to challenge it becomes severely compromised? When this happens, the PC can become a real threat to our mental health and well-being. This occurs when we suffer from bouts of depression or struggle with significant general or social anxiety or other mental-health difficulties. It is also the most likely source of the negative internal voice in eating disorders such as anorexia nervosa, berating us if we do not starve ourselves. We now have a formidable enemy on our hands! The PC can also thrive in the new medium of the twenty-first century, namely social media.

The Pathological Critic, Adolescents and Social Media

Our modern culture with its obsession with Facebook, Instagram, Snapchat and other social-media platforms has inadvertently opened the PC to a whole new world of opportunity. Social media built on the essential principles of self- and other-rating is meat and drink to it. This is because the torrent of abuse and negative criticism and judgements pouring in through these mediums is adding to the negative vibes from our PC. As adults, busy playing the rating game online, this is bad enough. But for our vulnerable adolescents, whose PC is usually overactive to begin with, the effects can often be extremely damaging. Their immature brains, in a stage of transformation, lack the critical overview provided by the mature rational brain of the adult. In these situations, the PC may become dominant and tip the young person into the worlds of anxiety, depression and self-harm.

The opportunities presented by social media to feed the PC include issues to do with image, bullying, mocking, taunting, isolation from peer groups, body image such as fat shaming and many more. It is like feeding a monster who thrives on the diet and grows into a greater menace. The deadly trio of social media, the smartphone and the PC are destroying the mental health and peace of mind of many of our young people. Add to that the well-meaning attempts to protect our children and boost their self-esteem and we have the makings of the current mental-health epidemic being experienced throughout many parts of the developed world. The earlier we give young people a smartphone and allow them on to such platforms, the more we allow the monster which the PC can become to thrive.

This is not because it is damaging their self-esteem, as many have claimed. It is more that it encourages them down the road of negative personal self-rating. We will explore later how some adolescents and young adults, struggling with the negative bullying effects of social media and the inner critic, can learn new ways to face down the PC.

The Language of the Pathological Critic

You may not recognise the role the PC is playing in your emotional mind. You may be unaware of the language it is using, or you may only become aware of this voice if something extremely negative occurs in your life.

But imagine if someone rang you every day at 9.00 a.m. and informed you in no uncertain terms that you were:

- A failure
- Useless
- Stupid
- Weird/odd/abnormal
- Weak
- Boring
- Worthless
- Ugly

Clearly, if one encountered this voice at the end of a phone on a constant slow-drip basis, the damage to your morale would be profound. The danger is that eventually you would begin to believe that this 'close friend' must be telling you the truth you don't want to hear – namely that you are indeed all the above. You would then tend to become increasingly anxious or depressed emotionally. You do have the capacity in the case of such a friend, however, to change your phone number and switch off this nasty tirade.

But when it comes to our internal critic, it is not so simple. Our emotional mind is very strong and tends to overpower us when not in a good space from a mental-health perspective. So, if our PC begins to dominate us, we may be receiving these negative messages constantly throughout the day, destroying our peace of mind and putting our mental health under severe pressure. This can be the case, for example, when going through a difficult period in adolescence, experiencing a bout of depression, or significant social or general anxiety, or struggling with body-image issues or sexual identity. In such scenarios, our rational or logical mind is silenced. We will be exploring in the next chapter how best to challenge our PC when it has become dominant in this manner. We do so by harnessing the power of our rational mind. More about this later.

The above list of negative self-descriptions used by the PC is only a 'flavour' of the language it can use to flagellate us. It has a rich vocabulary and is extremely inventive. Some inform me that its favourite term is to inform them that they are 's**t'! It really is a nasty fellow.

How Does the Pathological Critic Work?

It is worth exploring how your PC gets away with its antics. Surely we are rational creatures who should be adept at putting this critical voice back into his/her box? Is this not why we have a logical or rational brain in the first place? Is its job not to put manners on the PC? Oh, if only it were so simple!

There are three characteristics that define the PC, which explains why it is so adept at making us miserable:

1. It is *vague*. This means that it speaks in generalities, never giving us specific information about what it is accusing us of. The typical example is: 'You are weak.' It is not providing us with much information here!
2. It is a *bully*. This means that it gets its way by brute force, crushing all opposition. We are just cannon fodder – to be mocked and put down without mercy. It also suggests that the PC is getting away with such behaviour as we lack the skills to challenge it.
3. It talks *nonsense*! If we were to forensically analyse much

of what the PC tries to get us to believe, this would become quickly apparent. Alas, this rarely happens.

To explain how the critic works in practice, I often use the following analogy with patients. I ask them to visualise a factory floor where the supervising manager is a known bully. He is lord of his kingdom and all kowtow to him at every available opportunity. Eventually, he drags this poor lad in front of the female CEO of the company and gleefully explains that 'he is a complete failure' and sits back to see what will happen. Maybe he is going to get the sack!

The CEO then asks the manager: 'Can you explain further? Why is he a failure?'

The manager puffs up his shoulders and replies arrogantly, 'I don't think it is a good idea to challenge my opinion. He is just a failure!'

The CEO, slightly irritated by this reply, then asks the lad himself, 'What do you have to say about this accusation?'

The young man, looking fearfully at the manager who is glaring at him, says, 'If he says I am a failure, I must be a failure!'

The CEO has had enough. 'But what were you meant to have failed at?' she enquires. 'Where is the evidence? Have you been making some significant mistakes on the factory floor?'

This leads to the manager being side-lined as the truth about what was happening down on the ground finally becomes clear. The manager who had tried to bully the poor lad ended up being put back firmly in his place.

This is an allegory to explain the balance of power in our mind when the PC is trying to drag us down to his level.

1. The CEO is our rational mind, emanating from higher structures in the brain.

2. The manager is the PC, the bully who is trying to rule our emotional mind. Its invective is emanating primarily from the emotional brain.
3. The employee is us!

If we try to challenge the PC or bully in our emotional mind, we are destined to lose the battle. The CEO is sitting in her office, unaware of what is going on down on the factory floor. We are therefore in for a relentless barrage of criticism from the PC, who is delighted to make us feel miserable with his vague snide remarks. The CEO is unable to protect us.

But when we write down on paper what the PC is saying – such as 'I am a failure' – the CEO, or our rational brain, can now challenge the content of such a statement and seek evidence as to its veracity. The CEO will want to know 'just what did you fail at?' She will be seeking evidence, not just vague hearsay. This is one of my core messages: the power of the written word over the ramblings of our emotional mind.

Once we understand how powerful and destructive the PC can be in real life and yet how it can be challenged and faced down, we are laying the foundations for how best to challenge self-rating and replace it with unconditional self-acceptance.

Where does the Pathological Critic Reside in the Brain?

This was a question posed to me by a perceptive patient following a discussion on the role of the PC. It is important as it is the rational part of the brain which is being side-lined and the emotional part of the brain that is unleashing the PC's venom. It is also of great relevance to those who struggle with bouts of depression, where the PC is rampant.

We are slowly moving away from an earlier model of trying to assign different functions to specific areas of the emotional and logical brain to one that sees the brain as an organ which is rapidly shifting information from area to area. The prefrontal cortex at the front of the brain is the key part of our rational and social brain. The limbic system, in the middle of the brain, relates more to the emotional part. Both are in constant and interactive communication, some of which is now felt to be in part caused by wave formations as well as through neurocircuitry connections.

It would take another book to examine all the potential areas of the emotional and logical brain that assist us to be self-critical. But I would like to briefly discuss a system called the Default Mode Network (DMN), which is increasingly seen as a key player in how we introspect. This was an area that was found to 'come alive' when we cease performing specific tasks, but on further exploration was found to be an essential component in our capacity to daydream and self-reflect. It contained many structures involved in our management of emotional and contextual memories. It also involves areas of both the limbic system and lower levels of the prefrontal cortex (PFC).

It has also been shown to be very important when we begin to ruminate or constantly and negatively self-critically flagellate ourselves over apparent faults, as during bouts of major depression. A colleague, Professor Philippe Fossatti from Paris, and others have been at the forefront of trying to explore which systems underlie this distressing cognitive symptom. They point to increased interconnectivity between the DMN and a key junction point between the emotional and logical brain as one of the drivers of the ruminations so prevalent in depression. For those interested in exploring in detail the role of this fascinating system, see the bibliography.

Since it is widely recognised that the PC is especially rampant during bouts of depression, with relentless negative self-criticism, it would point to this system as being one possible source of the critic. We are, however, only at the beginning of understanding such interactions between the brain and the mind. Much of our current ideas are still speculative in nature.

The Power Struggle

Before leaving this chapter, it is worth reflecting that to achieve unconditional self-acceptance, to be free of the chains of self-rating, to put to bed the myth of self-esteem, we are going to have to overcome a powerful enemy. One that wants to enslave us. One that wants us to feel anxious, depressed or ashamed. Namely our PC. But the PC, if active in your life, will not be easily overcome. So, if you wish to join me and march towards a goal of freedom and mental health, you may find yourself engaged in a power struggle. To develop unconditional self-acceptance, as we will now explore in the next chapter, the PC must often be subjugated. There can be only one winner: you, your peace of mind and mental health; or the PC. The choice will ultimately be yours.

6. UNCONDITIONAL
SELF-ACCEPTANCE

Let's return to our earlier discussion on Ellis and his strongly held viewpoint that many mental-health difficulties were created by our propensity to place 'conditions' on whether we were acceptable or not to ourselves as human beings. As Ellis rightly pointed out, there are limitless 'conditions' that we can place on ourselves to prevent us from becoming comfortable in our own skins. These can range from 'I must never fail at anything' to 'I must never make a mistake', 'I must be perfect in every way', 'Everyone must like me' – the list goes on and on!

But why do we think like this? Why do we make such demands? Why do we play the rating game? Why do we believe for example that we are worthless? Once again, Ellis comes to our rescue.

Irrational and Rational Beliefs

Ellis believed that all of us developed ways of thinking about the world which were rational or irrational. He called these 'rational' and 'irrational' beliefs. The former were sensible, logical and assisted us in getting on with our lives. The latter were illogical, problem causing and led to unhappiness and emotional difficulties.

It was his view that such beliefs were picked up like viruses as we interacted with our environment as children, adolescents and later in adult life. It was our irrational beliefs that led us to make impossible demands of ourselves, others and life. These irrational beliefs would then stick to us like limpets and re-emerge every time something negative happened to us in life.

Like a broken record, we were then doomed to repeat these negative patterns, unless we changed them. When an irrational belief was triggered, it would lead to negative emotions like anxiety, depression, shame, guilt, frustration or hurt, for example. These in turn would lead to unhealthy behavioural patterns. These irrational beliefs would become embedded into key parts of our emotional and logical brain, becoming difficult to shift without targeted cognitive and behavioural exercises.

When we find ourselves playing the rating game, we are usually triggering an underlying irrational belief. If I am listening to my PC and believing that 'I am worthless', for example, then I have triggered such an irrational belief. My corresponding emotion might be depression. If I am feeling ashamed as I believe that 'I must accept other people's rating', then I am also triggering an irrational belief.

If on the other hand I begin to believe that 'I must be perfect' or 'the world must change to suit me because I am the greatest', then I am triggering different but equally destructive irrational beliefs that will lead to emotions such as anxiety and frustration. This is because I am unable to achieve such impossible demands.

How to Achieve Unconditional Self-acceptance?

Many of you will recognise some of the unhealthy thinking patterns noted above – 'that's me all right!' – but despair at ever being able to break free from the relentless world of self-criticism and self-rating. Many of you will have come to accept the myth that you have 'low self-esteem' and are doomed to remain like this for the rest of your lives. I am often asked for assistance to boost a person's self-esteem as they assume this is the source of their mental-health difficulties.

You may recognise how often you are allowing other people to rate and judge you and believe that you must accept such judgements. Or you may be struggling to keep up with relentlessly high personal self-ratings that you have set. You would love to get off the treadmill and just be yourself, but don't know how to achieve this. Perhaps you have defined yourself as having high self-esteem in the past, but in private will often admit how little it is assisting you in your life and would love to discover a different path.

You are not doomed to continue inexorably down the path of rating for life. There is another road. One that will lead to deep-seated inner peace and contentment. One that is infinitely more challenging than simply sitting in the corner feeling anxious or depressed because one believes, for example, that one is 'useless' or 'a failure'. A road that will lead to genuine positive mental health. It is the road of unconditional self-acceptance.

Ellis's Insights

Let's return to what Ellis said about unconditional self-acceptance in chapter four. How he recommended to therapists that the 'real solution to the problem of "self-esteem"' was to give their clients 'unconditional acceptance'. That they should learn to define themselves as '"good", just because they are alive and human' and learn to 'rate only the effectiveness of their behaviour, while not rating their self, their being or their essence' (Ellis, 1996).

We can distil this wonderful message, which we will call 'Ellis's insights' into two sentences:

1. We must accept ourselves completely as human beings, without any preconditions, in a non-judgemental, non-rating manner.
2. We must also be prepared to both rate and take active responsibility for our behaviour or actions.

What Ellis teaches us is that we must learn to accept ourselves without conditions, while remaining free to rate and challenge our behaviour.

This latter concept has great significance for our modern world. Many of us spend our lives matching up to some illusory idea of who we or others think we should be, and so find ourselves anxious, depressed or ashamed.

But this irrational belief has another hidden negative consequence. It prevents us from seriously analysing where we might be failing in terms of our everyday behaviour and skills. It can promote an attitude of hopelessness: there is no point in me trying to move forward. I may believe my PC, who is convincing me that I am a failure. Because this now defines me in my own mind as being a failure as a human being, it can prevent me from analysing my behaviour and skills and seeing where I can improve.

I believe that we would all benefit from parking self-esteem and concentrating instead on living our lives based on Ellis's insights. All of us play the rating game. We need to be kinder to ourselves, stop living in the world of rating and simply accept responsibility for our behaviour. This is true self-acceptance, a skill worth learning and practising. I have seen this concept revolutionise lives. Every time I see a life transformed or a troubled person healed through the power of unconditional self-acceptance, I give thanks to the vision of Ellis, who has shown us the path to follow.

But how can you develop and put unconditional self-acceptance into practice? Like most skills, it is easy to learn and understand the concepts behind it, but difficult to put it into practice. In the following section we will show you how to achieve this with a simple but profound Unconditional Self-acceptance exercise. Let's now explore what this exercise involves and how to apply it in two situations. The first relates to those who are self-raters.

The Self-raters

This term refers to those who are constantly rating themselves, either up or down, depending on what is happening in our lives at that moment. Some of you may tend to mark yourselves in at the lower end of the rating scale, when faced with negative situations. You are the low self-raters.

The low self-raters

If you tend to fall into the trap of low self-rating when something negative occurs in your life, I suggest performing the following Unconditional Self-acceptance exercise.

1. For the next three months, carry a notebook around with you.
2. Whenever you start rating yourself, write down the trigger and what your PC is telling you about yourself. The typical trigger might involve somebody at work, or a family member or friend criticising something you have said or done.

3. Later in the day, when you are free to do so, write down on paper what the PC is telling you. It may be, for example, that you are a failure, useless, or worthless.

4. Then, on paper, challenge what the Pathological Critic is telling you, using techniques which we will now explore.

How to Challenge Your Pathological Critic

One of the short cuts to developing unconditional self-acceptance, especially if you are a low self-rater, is to challenge your internal critic using Ellis's insights as a guide. As already observed, your emotional mind is much more powerful than your logical mind. If the Pathological Critic is pouring out its venom, it is difficult to challenge it in your emotional mind. But on writing down its 'comments' on paper as detailed above, your logical mind can now challenge the content as follows.

'I am useless'

Suppose the PC's observation is that you are useless, and you wish to dispute this on paper. You would ask the following five questions:

1. What does this statement mean in practice?
2. Can I or indeed any human being be defined as 'useless' or indeed 'useful'?
3. Is this not just another attempt to rate myself as a person?
4. Is this belief preventing me from exploring some facet of my skills or behaviour that I might be less than useful at?
5. If this is the case, what can I learn from this analysis and how can I improve the situation for the future?

Now write down Ellis's two insights.

You will quickly see on paper that the statement 'I am useless' is a form of personal self-rating, so can be immediately discarded. Can a human being be defined as a 'useless' or 'useful' person? Of course not! However, you can certainly rate your behaviour or skills as useful or useless. If somebody wishes to assess or rate the latter, you are also free to debate with them whether this assessment is true or false. This enables you to distinguish between 'who you are as a human being' and 'your behaviour'. It also challenges you to assess areas of your skills or behaviour that may or may not require some input in terms of the future.

Imagine you are a teacher. Somebody makes a throwaway comment which implies you are a bad or useless teacher. Your PC takes over: maybe they are right, and I am useless! You find yourself emotionally feeling anxious and then later depressed. You write this down in your notebook and then later challenge it on paper as follows.

Your PC is implying that you are useless, which is of course another form of self-rating, as it suggests you are a useless person. But is this true? Can a human being be defined as a useless person? Of course not! By accepting this is not the case, you are now free to progress to an assessment of your teaching skills. Now you are on much safer ground. It is easier to debate on your strengths and weaknesses as a teacher. Has the incident highlighted, for example, some area of your practice that might benefit from some input? Or, on other occasions, you may feel that the comment about your teaching skills was inaccurate and you are then free to continue as before.

'I am weak'

So, too, with the belief that you are weak. Imagine not standing up for yourself when a work colleague challenges you. Later, your

PC begins to castigate you as being a weak person. You feel both depressed and ashamed that others would also have seen you as weak. Once again, you would write down the trigger and personal self-rating into your notebook. Later, you would dispute these using the five questions detailed on page 112 as a template to challenge your rating. Can a human being be rated as weak or strong? Is this yet again another form of personal self-rating? Can a human being be rated in this manner? Of course not.

Once again, you would also have to challenge your behaviour in relation to this occurrence. Do you need to upskill to learn how best to face down such an individual? If so, what actions are you going to take about this?

This approach would be healthier in a variety of ways. Many people who come to see me are convinced that they are 'weak' and long to be like others who, in their minds, are 'strong'. But what do such terms really mean when properly analysed on paper? I have never met anyone who does not demonstrate weaknesses in relation to some skills or behaviours and strengths in relation to others. We are an amalgam of the two, which is what makes us so different and unique. So, we can be 'weak at doing something' but cannot be a weak person. Neither can we be a 'strong' person for the same reasons. Some really struggle with the burden of this latter label. Everyone expects them to be 'the strong one' in every situation, usually an impossible task, and one that can also put their mental health under threat.

The other major benefit is that if we do find ourselves struggling with some weakness in a skill or behaviour, it opens the opportunity of learning how to improve in relation to these areas. This is an exciting possibility, denied to us if we simply sit in the corner feeling despondent and irrationally believing that we are a weak person.

If, for example, I believe that 'I am weak' as I am extremely over-weight and feeling depressed because of this personal self-rating, then I have two choices. The first is to believe that this belief is true and that I am a weak person. In this scenario, I am not required to make any further effort to try to tackle the issue. I may even find myself eating more, as I feel emotionally depressed secondarily to my negative self-rating. I have boxed myself in as being a weak person.

The second choice is to accept myself as the wonderful, special, unique person that I am but choose to challenge my current dietary and exercise regimens. Instead of trying to increase my self-esteem or self-rating, I can choose instead to accept myself as I am but take responsibility for my behaviour. A much healthier option!

'I am a failure'

Apart from 'I am weak', the commonest form of self-rating I encounter relates to the belief that 'I am a failure'. This is the PC at his best. For real life is steeped with opportunities for failure. It is an innate part of the human condition to fail – and to do so regularly and usually, in the case of the author, in style! Some of our young people unfortunately assume success relates to how big a profile one has online. How popular is your social-media platform presence? Are you a social-media influencer? Are you famous (even if only famous for being famous)? If not, then you may begin to see yourself as a failure. Whatever your definition of success or failure is, if it involves personal self-rating, you are in trouble.

A classic example might be where we fail at a specific task in relation to some area of our life. The PC swoops in: 'Not only are you completely useless, but also an abject failure.' You then see yourself as the failure. This in turn can lead to emotions of anxiety or depression. As above, you would write in your notebook the trigger and your personal self-rating. Later, on paper, you would dispute this irrational belief, using the five questions detailed on page 112 as a template to challenge your rating as follows.

Can a human being be a success or a failure as a person? If you believe this to be true, where is your evidence? What scale are you using to decide who is the success and who is the failure? The commonest answer in relation to success is that those with a good job, healthy relationship, plenty of money or a fine house seem to fit the bill. But are these genuine characteristics of each one of us as a person, or to do with how successful we are or not at acquiring the above? Should they not be a reflection of the hard work and effort put into achieving these desired outcomes? In this scenario they relate back to your skills and behaviour.

So, too, with failure. Can you be a failure as a person? The answer is clearly no, as this is a form of personal self-rating. But I can clearly fail at a task I have set myself, at a moment in time. I could, for example, set myself the task of achieving high marks in an exam but – as is often the case, often through no fault of our own – the paper set does not suit me and my mark is lower than expected. This does not mean you are a failure as a person. Rather, that you failed at the task set. The real key to failure lies in the next sentence. 'The only failure in life is not getting back up again.'

This is of course unconditional self-acceptance in real action. I will not rate myself as a person, no matter whether I do well or badly in a task or exam. But I am obliged to explore where errors might have been made and, if appropriate, decide how best to avoid these in the future. Instead of giving up and classifying myself as a failure, which is my PC's goal, I can now challenge and learn from mistakes or failures in terms of my skills or behaviour. Instead of assuming I fail at tasks because I have low self-esteem or rating myself as a failure if I do fail, I must accept that failure and mistakes are an integral part of life, ensure that I learn from them and do my best not to perpetuate them. Think how resilient our current crop of adolescents would become if this became their new mantra.

'I am worthless'

Another common cause of self-flagellation driven by the PC is the belief that 'I am worthless'. This is harking back yet again to the flawed world of self-esteem, where it is assumed that you as a human being can measure or value yourself as a person. This belief is especially common in those struggling with clinical depression, but also in other conditions such as general anxiety and eating disorders.

Of all the nasty vitriolic outpourings out of the PC, this is right up there as one of the most distressing statements we can make about ourselves. The implication is that you have little or no value as a human being. This is the delusion of self-worth fully expressing itself. We mentioned the term 'worth' in earlier chapters and how we struggled to define what it is, never mind measure it.

Once again, this irrational belief may be triggered by a small negative incident occurring in our everyday lives. It could be a response to someone busy passing us in the street. Off goes our PC: 'No wonder they passed me by. Aren't I worthless anyway, so why would they stop?'

As before, you would write in your notebook the trigger and your rating of yourself as being worthless as a person. Later, on paper, you would dispute this clearly irrational belief, using the five questions detailed on page 112 to challenge your rating as follows.

Can a human being be defined as being worthless as a person? The answer is a resounding 'no'. For, as explored in earlier chapters, if you say that 'you' are 'worth less', then this must suggest that someone else is 'worth more'. Human beings cannot be measured in such a manner. Mental-health difficulties arise when we believe that we can rate ourselves in this manner. It is the ultimate form of personal self-rating and one we must always forcefully challenge.

'I am weird'

The term 'weird' is a term in vogue amongst many adolescents, especially girls. Adults may prefer the terms 'abnormal', 'odd' or 'different'. The belief that 'I am weird/abnormal' abounds in social anxiety but can also be present in general anxiety and depression. There are countless people who can relate to this irrational belief and it can make their lives a misery. It suggests that 'I, as a human being, am abnormal, different, odd or weird' and is another example of the PC running riot. It can lead to emotions of depression and shame.

A typical example might be where you feel uncomfortable in a social situation and develop physical symptoms that you believe (incorrectly) others might see and as a result you assume they will think you are weird! You would write down the trigger and personal self-rating in your notebook and later challenge it on paper, using the five questions on page 112, as follows.

Can a human being be classified as being odd or weird? On what grounds or how would you measure which amongst us is 'normal' (whatever that is) or 'abnormal' as a human being?

The answer to the first question is, of course, no! For human beings cannot be rated in such a manner. There is simply no scale to do so. We are left with only one other possibility. Can our behaviour be abnormal or weird or odd? The answer is yes. If I am drunk and staggering down the street and weaving my way in front of traffic, is my behaviour abnormal? Yes, this behaviour would be considered abnormal or odd. So, you as a person are not abnormal or weird, it is only your behaviour that could be considered as such.

We would end up disputing this statement on paper as above and using Ellis's insights to challenge its validity. It could on occasion also lead me to assess and do something to improve my abnormal behaviour. This might involve reducing my alcohol intake in the example quoted. Again, a healthier alternative.

'I am stupid'

The last example is another common belief that the PC is delighted to share with us. How often do we mess up in relation to something and find ourselves lacerating ourselves with the inner critical thought, 'I am stupid'?

It may be that you made some simple error in your everyday life, such as forgetting a loved one's birthday, or messed up in relation to routine finances, or forgot to email someone at work – the list is endless. The PC swiftly moves into action, happy to inform you that 'you are stupid'. This makes you feel emotionally depressed. You would write down the trigger and personal self-rating into your notebook. Later, you would dispute these, using the five questions detailed on page 112 to challenge your negative personal self-rating.

Can a human being be rated in such a manner? Can we really divide human beings into two types, one regarded as 'stupid' and the other 'clever'?

Once again, this would make no sense, as would quickly become apparent. Human beings are too special and complex to be defined in such a global manner. Since human beings are easily distracted, each one of us can relate to making such common mistakes. We can certainly rate our intellectual or practical skills as greater or lesser than another person but not who we are as individual human beings. I could be a clever accountant but quite stupid at reading social cues, for example. Neither statement describes who I am as a human being: they are just assessments of my skills or behaviour. If we did discover some areas of our skills or behaviour that we could work on or improve, then this would be a sensible road to travel.

Underlying the above situations is a common trend. In each case the PC is trying to make us believe in some vague general, personal self-rating belief, that we are weak, useless, a failure, stupid or worthless. As a bully, it knows just the buttons to press! But if we are prepared to dig in and spend three or four months performing the above Unconditional Self-acceptance exercise, the results can be life-changing. Your emotional resilience will soar. Your mental health and well-being will be greatly nurtured and strengthened. You are now on a path to true inner peace and contentment. You will become 'comfortable in your own skin'.

As with all skills, however, when life produces challenging situations, the tendency will be to revert to normal negative patterns. In such situations you may find yourself reverting to listening to your PC, rather than facing him down on paper. If this occurs, a month or so of the Unconditional Self-acceptance exercise will quickly put you back on track.

The High Self-raters

There is another group who rarely struggle with low personal self-rating but tend to assess themselves highly on the rating scale.

They tend to blame others or the situation they find themselves in if something negative occurs. These are the high self-raters. This group cannot cope with the possibility that something they have done may be the issue as this would conflict with the high opinion they have of themselves as a person. Instead of becoming anxious or depressed, they tend to become frustrated and angry when matters are not going their way. We will be meeting some who fit into this picture later in the book.

In this scenario, the person often becomes frustrated with themselves or the situation: it is the situation which is the problem, not me! But they can also become disturbed as their inner critical voice implies that it 'expects more from them' due to their excessively high personal self-rating.

In other scenarios, the PC can get the odd jibe in that 'you should be reaching the lofty heights that you have set for yourself', with once again an implied self-criticism. This can drive the person to strive even harder to achieve the high personal self-ratings they have set, leading to mental-health consequences. Or the PC may suggest that their natural state is to be a 'success', which puts even further pressure on them to succeed, with resulting negative consequences.

It is as if the PC is working in reverse. Instead of implying we are a failure, as in those who tend to be low self-raters, it does the opposite. It suggests that we as human beings are the greatest, a success, and worth more than others. Clearly such beliefs are setting us up for a fall.

Many who fall into these high self-rating categories tend in my experience to fiercely object to Ellis's insights. They tend to 'live for their ratings' and struggle to accept that such ratings are not helping them in their lives. They, like a monkey with a nut, may refuse to let go of their excessively high personal self-ratings, even if such beliefs are irrational and damaging to their mental health.

Apart from the above group, who make up the majority of this category, some perfectionists may also be high self-raters. They demand impossibly high standards, so tend to rate themselves highly on the rating scale. They can become emotionally anxious if they cannot be 100 per cent certain they can achieve such perfect standards, or on other occasions extremely frustrated with themselves if they do end up making errors. In the case of the former, where they become anxious, the PC may once again attempt to convince them that they are failures. For such an individual, a drop from 95 on the rating scale down to 70 is catastrophic.

If you recognise yourself in the above, I suggest you too perform the Unconditional Self-acceptance exercise for three months. If you struggle with extreme frustration with yourself or anxiety if you are unable to reach your high personal self-ratings, this exercise may be extremely helpful. When something negative happens, write down the trigger and the emotion, whether it be frustration, anxiety or depression, and any form of critical self-rating. Later, on paper, using the five questions detailed on page 112, challenge whether such ratings are helping you in your life or in practice upsetting your mental health and well-being.

Explore whether embracing Ellis's insights might be of greater assistance. Would dropping my high rating demands altogether allow me to become comfortable in my own skin and relieve much of the pressure I am placing on myself? Would it on occasion be more helpful to assess my behaviour or skills and take responsibility for errors made there, rather than for example trying to find something wrong with either the situation or those around me? Is this not more challenging and more effective at nurturing and growing my mental health?

The Other-raters

Perhaps you are someone who generally tends not to personally self-rate if something negative occurs. However, you may assign great importance as to how others rate you in certain situations. Is the Unconditional Self-acceptance exercise still of relevance? The answer is once again unquestionably yes.

This is because you are also falling into the trap of believing that a human being can be rated at all, by allowing others to rate you in this manner. Perhaps you have accepted in your mind the irrational belief that others should be given the power to judge you and that you must accept their judgement. If you can relate to this, then shame and embarrassment will be regular visitors in your life. Some readers may have picked up such beliefs from childhood, adolescence or early adult life and they are now embedded in their psyche.

The solution lies again in learning to accept Ellis's insights and applying them in your life. Practising the Unconditional Self-acceptance exercise for three months will assist you to do this. This is because when we decide that others think we are weak or weird or boring or stupid or worthless, we are indirectly triggering the PC into action, even though it is our belief that we are not rating ourselves. For why would believing such perceived judgements of others bother us at all otherwise? The PC can be sneaky, so is adept at twisting our belief that others can rate us negatively into a subtle indirect 'dig' at us personally. So, unconsciously, other-rating morphs into personal self-rating.

So when, during the three-month period, something triggers such beliefs, write down the trigger and the perceived rating that you believe others are applying to you in your notebook. Later, on paper, challenge the beliefs using the questions detailed earlier.

Can a human being be rated at all? If not, then why should I accept someone else's judgement of me as weak or weird, etc.? Is this not falling back into the trap of personal self- and other-rating? Rather, you can assess if they are rating some behaviour or skill you are attempting to perform. If so, you have the right to decide on paper if such an assessment is accurate or inaccurate and challenge it as appropriate. If you do discover some areas of your skills or behaviour that could use some tweaking, then you must take responsibility for making the relevant changes.

A Good Rule of Thumb

There may be a fortunate few who have already developed and regularly practise unconditional self-acceptance in their daily lives. In my own experience, I have encountered precious few who are genuinely comfortable in their own skins. Most of us will fall into one of the three groups identified above.

A good rule of thumb is that most of us would benefit greatly by identifying which group we belong to and applying the appropriate Unconditional Self-acceptance exercise for three months as laid out above.

Before dismissing this suggestion outright as unnecessary in your case, do take a good hard look at the 'high-rater' section.

Now let's explore how others, coming from the three strands discussed above, learned how to put the above exercise into practice in different domains and situations encountered during their busy lives.

Many readers may see themselves in some of the cases described and find it helpful to see how those affected banish the myth of self-esteem and the flawed concept of self- and other-rating and learn to embrace instead the principles of unconditional self-acceptance.

7. UNCONDITIONAL SELF-ACCEPTANCE AND EDUCATION

Why Education?

One may justifiably ask: why focus on the role of self-acceptance in education? The answer is that the adolescent period between thirteen and twenty-five is where most mental-health difficulties begin, some of which may affect the person for the rest of their life.

We have strongly debunked the myth that self-esteem has any role to play in preparing our young people for life, and yet traits of this delusion are still lurking in the background of education. The many challenges education presents do unfortunately form the perfect breeding ground for personal self-rating and other-rating, increasing significantly risks of depression, anxiety, self-harm, suicide, eating disorders and addiction – subjects we will be dealing with later.

It is therefore important to introduce the concept of unconditional self-acceptance as early as possible in the education cycle, especially in primary school and early to mid-teens onwards, as a bulwark to protect our children from the many pitfalls that they can fall into. This goes back to what should be the real goal of education. Not to fill their heads with knowledge or to achieve high academic targets. But to prepare our children and adolescents for real life.

Unconditional Self-acceptance and Primary Education

It would be remiss not to mention the role of unconditional self-acceptance in the primary-school sector. Teaching children as early as possible to cease rating themselves but encouraging them instead to take responsibility for their actions, could transform their future lives.

This is a radical, revolutionary concept and one that I believe could be done in an age-appropriate manner. But it does require teachers, principals and parents to embrace the concept themselves and to share it with children wherever possible. My colleague Enda Murphy is at the forefront of trying to spearhead such an objective in Ireland.

There are many obstacles to be surmounted to achieve such a goal. State educational and psychological services are built on and woven around the concept of self-esteem and how best to boost it. And yet many teachers and principals express unease at how ineffective this approach has been in real life. We have already explored the reasons underlying this.

The experts will require years of research and pilot projects before even discussing whether such a simple idea could or should be introduced into primary schools. However, I cannot see any negatives to teaching a child (in an age-appropriate manner) to become comfortable with themselves, to cease judging themselves and others and to learn to take full responsibility for their behaviour. Is this not the essence of teaching a child good mental health and encouraging emotional resilience?

There is also the issue for principals and teachers in schools of how best to bring parents with them on such a project. It is hard to teach a child unconditional self-acceptance at school if the parents are not on board.

The ethos of the school needs to promote such ideas. Unconditional Self-acceptance would need to underpin every aspect of school life. There might be a concern that this would interfere with normal education. But because it involves accepting responsibility for their behaviour, it does not let the child off the hook. Rather, it challenges them to do their best and to be rewarded for the efforts they put into achieving results in relation to all aspects of school life, not just academia. This may involve introducing them to the reality of failure when their best efforts come up short. But also to the concept that the only failure in life is not getting back up and trying again. Perhaps if this became embedded in the psyche of our children in primary school, we might see fewer problems arising at secondary and tertiary levels!

The Exam-pressure Years

Let's now focus on that turbulent period between the late teens and mid-twenties when most of the difficulties arise. This covers the period of doing final secondary school exams and attending tertiary education. We will refer to this phase as the 'Exam-pressure Years'.

It is a time of maximum stress and pressure for many young people and indeed their families and loved ones. Our current education model, whether at school or college, is built on results or grades, especially in the UK, Ireland and USA. This model favours the more academic child, placing increased pressure on both them and those less academically driven. This can create significant mental-health difficulties, as already discussed.

The challenges

Some common challenges which young people face during the phase include:

1. The pressure to achieve certain grades in exams to be able to advance into tertiary level courses which would allow them to engage in a career, skill or vocation.
2. The major pressure they are experiencing, either stated or implied, from well-meaning parents who want them to do well in life.
3. The difficulties faced by those students who are not academically driven but who have other talents often un-noticed or validated by themselves, their parents and on occasions even their teachers.
4. The difficulties young people may face on arriving at a tertiary level college in adjusting socially and otherwise, whilst also fulfilling the requirement to self-discipline themselves to study for their course.
5. The major issue which often arises when realising that they are on the wrong course, and the pressure and shame of revealing this to parents.
6. The struggles that those with lesser academic skills experience to achieve their objectives at secondary or college exams.
7. The separate challenges that the high-achieving perfectionist students must overcome to achieve their objectives. This might include their natural tendency to procrastinate.

Unconditional self-acceptance and the exam-pressure years

This is where learning unconditional self-acceptance and putting it into practice in your life can bear much fruit for students, parents and educators.

Perhaps you are a student who is falling into the trap of self-rating in relation to education. Are you setting the rating bar too high and struggling with anxiety or frustration when matters academic are not working out as you had envisaged? Maybe you are setting the rating bar too low if results are not going your way and you end up feeling anxious or depressed? Or you may be allowing others such as parents or peers to rate you and become anxious or ashamed if you are struggling academically. None of these approaches assist us in our lives but tend to do the opposite by making us anxious, depressed or ashamed.

If you are a young person caught up in playing this rating game, especially during final secondary school exams or your first few years at college, then this chapter may help you to reshape your thinking and behaviour. It will show you how to separate who you are as a person from your responsibilities as a student. This will have the added advantage of helping you get the best out of yourself academically whilst growing into a more contented, mature and reflective adult.

If you are a parent, there are important messages to be learned as to how best to assist your adolescent and young adult students to be more effective and resilient during this turbulent and often difficult decade. Education must be more than just achieving high academic standards. It must prepare us for real life. Encourage your child or young adult to develop true unconditional self-acceptance, and you will greatly assist them to achieve both goals. It goes without saying that you must firstly learn and practise the skill yourself and only then try to pass it on to them.

If you are a secondary or tertiary level teacher or lecturer, there is also much to be gained by reading this chapter and encouraging your students to achieve unconditional self-acceptance. But you too must buy into the concept by developing it in yourself as a person first and only then as a professional.

If you can see yourself or someone you love struggling with some of these scenarios, then read on. For we are now going to meet a group of individual students who have encountered many of the challenges noted above and see how embracing unconditional self-acceptance changed their lives for the better.

Peter's story

Peter, an eighteen-year-old student, is beginning his final year at school. Coming from a family of sibling high achievers, he struggled to live in their shadow. He had suffered from anxiety from an early age, like his mother, who hid her fears and worries from her children lest it 'infected' them. Like her, he tended to constantly worry and catastrophise, often over seemingly small setbacks. His father, a highly successful but unempathetic businessman, expected big things from his children, making them aware of this at every opportunity. Whilst his two siblings had coped fine, Peter struggled to match up to his father's high expectations.

He was holding it together until his final year at school, when it all started to unravel. He became increasingly physically anxious. His emotional mind took over as he constantly catastrophised as to how poorly he was going to perform in his final exams and how upset his father would be when this happened. Then panic attacks arrived and it became a challenge to even make it into school. This made him increasingly anxious. What was he going to do now? He gradually began to fall further behind in his studies, leading him to catastrophise more.

His parents then attended their family doctor with Peter in tow. His mother explained that Peter was suffering from anxiety and wondered if he could talk to someone about his difficulties. His father insisted that Peter had always suffered from low self-esteem issues. Was some medication available to reduce his anxiety and boost his self-esteem? He explained that his other two children, like himself, have high self-esteem, which explained their academic success.

When Peter had a chance to speak to his GP alone, he explained how his panic attacks, academic difficulties and relationship with his father were making him anxious and on occasions emotionally depressed. He revealed he had considered self-harm as he was unable to see a path out of his current dilemma. 'I cannot cope with these panic attacks and spend my days constantly worrying about everything. Sometimes I just don't want to go on.' He too wondered if his self-esteem is low. 'Maybe my dad is right,' he added and queried as how best to boost it.

His family doctor reassured both Peter and his parents that this is simply anxiety and that he would refer him to a colleague, Dr Jim, 'to help deal with your anxiety and panic attacks and to manage your self-esteem issues'.

Dr Jim empathises with Peter's story, reassuring him that he will teach him some CBT methods and skills to manage his panic attacks and anxiety and to cope with what Peter and his father called 'self-esteem issues'. Peter is relieved that at last someone has understood and empathises.

Firstly, Dr Jim teaches Peter how to banish his panic attacks using a simple technique called Flooding (dealt with in detail in *Emotional Resilience* and *Anxiety and Panic*). This involves Peter learning to visualise that he is stuck to the ground when such episodes arise and going with (rather than trying to stop) the uncomfortable physical symptoms of the panic episode. Peter also learns that such episodes are of short duration and not dangerous in any way.

Peter is so relieved to know that his physical symptoms are due to an adrenaline rush. He begins to apply these techniques and within a few weeks they begin to settle. His panic attacks are no longer something that would worry him in the future as he now has a skill to deal with them.

Dr Jim then moves on to assist him in dealing with his anxiety issues.

He tells Peter about rational and irrational beliefs and lays out the ABC concepts, explaining how they will employ this system to locate and manage his irrational beliefs. He asks for a routine example of something that had previously triggered a bout of anxiety so that they can put together an ABC of this event.

Peter gives him an example that he regularly becomes anxious when he has an upcoming test. 'So, we now have the trigger which is the upcoming test and your emotion which is anxiety,' says Dr Jim, 'but how does the anxiety make you feel physically?' Peter explains that he suffers from 'fatigue, stomach in knots, muscles all tense, sleep difficulties and nightmares and constantly sighing'. On some occasions closer to the test, he notes, his heart would start thumping and his breathing would become fast and shallow.

'And what would you do when you become very anxious?' asks Dr Jim. Peter explains that 'he would worry and catastrophise about the test and how badly he would fail'. He also admits to swinging between over-studying on some occasions or delaying or procrastinating until it was almost too late on others. 'I am just a mess at these times,' he admits.

They put all this information down on Peter's ABC:

A – Activating Event:
- Trigger: upcoming test
- Inference/danger:

B – Belief/Demands:

C – Consequences:
- Emotional reactions: anxiety
- Physical reactions: stomach is in knots; sighing; fast, shallow breathing; heart beating a little faster; shaking; muscle tension; teeth-grinding and nightmares at night; and significantly increased tiredness and fatigue
- Behaviour: constantly worrying; catastrophising; over-studying or procrastinating

'So, what was it about your upcoming test that was making you feel anxious?' asks Dr Jim. 'What danger were you assigning to it?'

Peter replies that his major danger was that he would make a mess of the test. He also admits that he could visualise how upset his father would be if he kept failing tests. 'But my real danger is that I will make a mess of the final exams,' he admits.

'But why would that bother you?' persists Dr Jim.

'I would feel like such a failure,' he replies. 'I would also be concerned that I might not achieve the grades required for the course I want to do in college. I can just imagine how well that would go down with Dad,' he adds ruefully.

'So now let's examine what irrational belief was triggered by this situation and the danger you assigned to it,' says Dr Jim. 'This usually takes the form of some absolute demand you are making about the trigger.' With Dr Jim's help, Peter identifies that his main demand was that 'he must not fail the test or indeed his final exam. If this did happen, he would be a failure'.

They add this information to complete his ABC:

A – Activating Event:

- Trigger: upcoming test
- Inference/danger: he might fail his test; his father will be upset if this occurs; he might not do well enough in his final exam; if this happens, he might not make it to college; if this happens, his father will be upset and he, Peter, will feel he has failed

B – Belief/Demands: 'I must not fail my test. If this happens, I am a failure.' 'I must do well in my final exams and make it to college. If this does not happen, I am a failure.'

C – Consequences:

- Emotional reactions: anxiety
- Physical reactions: stomach is in knots; sighing; fast, shallow breathing; heart beating a little faster; shaking; muscle tension; teeth-grinding and nightmares at night; and significantly increased tiredness and fatigue
- Behaviour: constantly worrying; catastrophising; over-studying or procrastinating

Dr Jim then challenges Peter's thinking and behaviour.

They agree that his behaviour is not assisting the situation and is increasing rather than reducing his anxiety. It would have to change. They discuss his tendency to over-study and on occasions procrastinate and how unhelpful such behaviours are. Dr Jim gives him some advice in relation to both.

'Let's now examine and challenge your "B", or your irrational belief,' says Dr Jim. 'This took the form of an absolute demand that "you must not fail your test and must do well in your final exams. If not, you are a failure." Is this demand rational or irrational?' he inquires.

Peter agrees it is probably irrational.

Dr Jim then asks, 'What would be a healthier demand?'

After some discussion, they both agree that a more rational or healthier demand might be that 'He would prefer if he passed this or indeed any test but that this was out of his control.'

This leads to a discussion on the importance of control in Peter's life. Dr Jim asks him what he can really control in his life. After a few attempts to answer this, Peter realises that he can control very little. Dr Jim explains that when we are seeking control, one of the four things we are looking for is 100 per cent certainty. The other three are 100 per cent order, security and perfection. 'So, what were you looking for here?' asks Dr Jim.

'I was seeking 100 per cent certainty,' Peter replies. Following discussion, he accepts that it is unrealistic to demand 100 per cent certainty about this or indeed anything in life. To teach him how to challenge this demand, Dr Jim suggests that over the course of the next month, he performs the coin exercise detailed in *Emotional Resilience*. This would involve him listing areas of his daily life that he really enjoyed and then tossing a coin on each occasion as to whether he can participate in these activities or not. This is to introduce uncertainty into his daily life so that he would quickly learn how to cope and adapt to it when things did not go his way.

Dr Jim also teaches Peter skills to reduce his automatic tendency to catastrophise: for several months he must write down and challenge such conclusions on paper. They also agreed that if the worst-case scenario did occur and he did badly in his exams that there were other options open to him, such as repeating the exams or more sensibly finding a different route to arrive at the desired destination.

But Dr Jim is especially interested in challenging Peter's irrational belief that he would be a failure if the test did not go well. 'Would you be a failure or have simply failed at a specific task?'

he queries. He performs the Rating Exercise detailed earlier, with Peter noting how quickly his rating dropped if the scenario was created where he performed poorly in his test and how others' ratings of him would also plummet if this occurred.

After some discussion, however, both agree that there are no criteria to rate a human being. Dr Jim introduces the concept of unconditional self-acceptance, explaining Ellis's insights in detail – that Peter must cease rating or measuring himself as a human being whilst accepting responsibility for his behaviour.

Dr Jim explains that Peter's difficulties have little to do with self-esteem and all to do with his tendency to constantly rate himself and accept the judgements of others. They discuss the PC and how it was trying to bully Peter into believing he was a 'failure' or 'weak' or 'useless'. He quickly identifies this critical voice and vows to challenge the bully. He agrees to carry out the Unconditional Self-acceptance exercise detailed earlier for the following three months.

Dr Jim demonstrates how to challenge the PC on paper. He explains, for example, that 'he could fail at a task at a particular moment in time (i.e. an exam) but could not be a failure as a person as this was a form of personal rating which was now "off-limits"'. Peter is especially taken by the statement 'that the only failure in life was not getting back up again', vowing that this would become his new mantra.

Over the following months, because of the hard work put in in performing these exercises, Peter's life is transformed. His confidence grows. He learns to cease trying to control the world around him and accepts that uncertainty was an inevitable part of life. His panic attacks abate and his tendency to catastrophise greatly diminishes. But it is his hard work and perseverance in developing unconditional self-acceptance that really makes the difference. He no longer feels a need to 'match up' to his siblings and is even confident enough to gently challenge his father when the latter becomes too critical, advising his dad that 'it was the effort he was putting in rather than results that they should be discussing'. His father is beginning to get the message and become more encouraging. Peter also feels comfortable in dismissing any further discussion on the role of self-esteem in the house as irrelevant as human beings cannot be valued in such a manner.

By the time the exams came around, he was in a good space, surprising himself as to how calm he was during them. The good news, as he reported back to Dr Jim, was that he acquired enough points to enter his preferred course and was ready to face the fresh challenges of college life.

Emma's story

Emma is nineteen, a complete perfectionist who found herself struggling with anxiety during her first year of college. Every new assignment became another opportunity to procrastinate as her perfectionism switched on. She had always struggled with this trait. It controlled every aspect of her life from social media to her appearance, to the psychology course she was now embarking upon. A close friend had even suggested she was doing the course to find out about herself and there were times when she agreed.

Things came to a head when she received a lower grade in an assignment due to procrastinating until the last minute before finally completing and sending it in. She broke down in tears in front of her mum who suggested she seek out assistance to cope with her perfectionism-driven anxiety. Her mum intimated that she had inherited the trait from her dad, who responded more with frustration and annoyance than anxiety when things were not completely perfect.

Emma attends Dr Jim on the advice of the college counsellor, who also suggests that she may be suffering from self-esteem issues as well as perfectionism.

Dr Jim empathises with her story and suggests some CBT techniques to deal with both her perfectionism and her anxiety. He tells Emma about rational and irrational beliefs and lays out the ABC concepts, explaining how they will employ this system to locate and manage her irrational beliefs. They decide to use her most recent assignment as the trigger and note how her emotional response was anxiety. She also describes her typical physical anxiety symptoms of fatigue, tension headaches, sleep difficulties and bowel discomfort.

'And what did you do or what was your behavioural response to being anxious?' asks Dr Jim.

Emma admits to 'constantly delaying the assignment, only handing it in at the last minute', worrying about it constantly, and catastrophising that it would not be as perfect as she wished. She had stopped eating her normal meals, noticed some weight loss and dumped her normal exercise regime. She also tried to distract herself using social media and constantly sought reassurance from classmates and her mum. This was her routine behavioural pattern on becoming anxious.

They added this information to Emma's ABC:

A – Activating Event:
- Trigger: upcoming assignment
- Inference/danger:

B – Belief/Demands:

C – Consequences:

- Emotional reactions: anxiety
- Physical reactions: stomach is in knots; muscle tension; sleep difficulties; tension headaches; irritable bowel symptoms; and significantly increased tiredness and fatigue
- Behaviour: constantly worrying; catastrophising; procrastinating over doing and handing in her assignment; seeking reassurance; stopped eating and exercise; losing weight; distracting herself with social media

'So, what was it about this assignment that was making you feel anxious?' asks Dr Jim. 'What danger were you attributing to it?'

'That I would be unable to do it perfectly,' answers Emma.

'But why would it bother you if the completed assignment was not perfect?' he asks.

'Because then I would think I was a failure,' she replies, adding that, 'I expect more of myself. My standards have always been high. I cannot cope if unable to reach them. I was always a perfectionist, just like my dad,' she elaborates further. 'I cannot let the assignment go forward till I have rechecked it constantly to root out even the smallest imperfection.'

'So now let's examine what irrational belief was triggered by this situation and the danger you assigned to it,' says Dr Jim. 'This usually takes the form of some absolute demand you are making about the trigger.'

With Dr Jim's help, Emma identifies that her main demand was that 'she must hand in a perfect assignment; if not, she is a failure'.

They then add this information to complete her ABC:

A – Activating Event:
- Trigger: upcoming assignment

- Inference/danger: that the assignment would not be perfect, that she was a failure if it were not

B – Belief/Demands: 'My assignment must be perfect. If it is not, I am a failure.'

C – Consequences:

- Emotional reactions: anxiety
- Physical reactions: stomach is in knots; muscle tension; sleep difficulties; tension headaches; irritable bowel symptoms; and significantly increased tiredness and fatigue
- Behaviour: constantly worrying; catastrophising; procrastinating over doing and handing in her assignment; seeking reassurance; stopped eating and exercise; losing weight; distracting herself with social media; searching her work repeatedly, seeking out minor imperfections

They both agree that her unhealthy behaviours were not assisting her, and Emma agrees to work with Dr Jim to change them. He especially promises to assist her later in dealing with her procrastination and tendency to only seek out imperfections.

'Let's now examine and challenge your "B", or your irrational belief,' says Dr Jim. 'This took the form of an absolute demand that your assignment must be perfect. If not, you are a failure. Is this demand rational or irrational?' he inquires. Emma agrees it is probably irrational.

Dr Jim then asks, 'What would be a healthier demand?'

After some discussion, Emma agrees that a more rational or healthier demand might be that she would prefer if her assignment was perfect but that in real life this was out of her control. This leads to a discussion on the importance of control in Emma's life. Dr Jim asks her what she can really control in her life. After a few attempts to answer this, Emma realises that she can control very little.

Dr Jim explains that when we are seeking control, one of the four things we are looking for is 100 per cent certainty. Others include 100 per cent perfection, order and security.

'So, what were you looking for here?' asks Dr Jim.

'I was seeking 100 per cent certainty and especially 100 per cent perfection,' Emma replies.

Following discussion, she accepts that it was unrealistic to demand 100 per cent certainty about this or indeed anything in life. To challenge this demand, Dr Jim suggests that over the course of the following month she performs the coin exercise already detailed.

'But what about 100 per cent perfection?' asks Dr Jim. 'Is this possible in real life?' This leads to a frank conversation as to the irrationality of this demand. 'In real life,' he explains 'absolute perfection is impossible for any of us to achieve. There will always be some imperfections – however small.' He also explains how those of us who seek total perfection often fall into the trap of seeking out only imperfections in the world around us. We apply the same approach to assignments, constantly searching till we find some minor glitches whilst ignoring the fine work that has gone into the overall preparation.

To assist Emma to dampen down her demand for 100 per cent perfection, he suggests carrying out some perfectionism exercises detailed in *Emotional Resilience*. These would include messing up something in her appearance and social media daily for at least a month and having to live with these imperfections for twenty-four hours without changing them. By purposely creating imperfections and teaching her to adapt to them when present, he is dismantling her perfectionism.

His primary concern, however, was to assist her in challenging the belief that 'she is a failure' if the assignment was imperfect. They end up having a long discussion about the world of self-rating and how our PC can convince us that we are failures or worthless or useless, etc. Emma can easily relate to this inner critical voice. It had been a cruel but constant companion for as long as she could remember.

Dr Jim introduces her to Ellis's insights. Emma realises that her whole world has been built on shifting sands. She has always regarded herself as a failure, even admitting that she regularly believed she was worthless. She had always assumed that this meant she had low self-esteem but had been unsure as to how to boost it! It came as a huge relief that she was not indeed a failure or worthless as a person, but that it was quite acceptable to rate her skills or talents or behaviours.

She agrees to put the Unconditional Self-acceptance exercise into action for the following three months and enthusiastic about the prospect. Finally, Dr Jim gives her some tips on how to cease her procrastinating behaviour. This would involve (as discussed in *Emotional Resilience*) creating personal versus real-time deadlines, breaking tasks into three parts and assigning equal times to complete each third. Then handing the assignment in well ahead of the deadline date.

Three months later, Emma is thriving. She has ceased rating herself as a person and is now comfortable in her own skin. She has also learned to accept the imperfections of life and regularly applies her procrastination exercises to each new assignment with great results. Her anxiety levels have plummeted and she has found that the less she demands 100 per cent perfection, the higher her grades climb, a true paradox. Most of all she has dumped the unhealthy worlds of self-esteem and self-rating and replaced them with the gift of unconditionally loving and accepting herself as the special and unique person she is.

Michael's story

Michael's story is unfortunately an all too familiar one for many students, parents and colleges. He is twenty and finds himself trapped in a course that he absolutely hates. He had always been uncertain of what to do with his life. When choosing to take a science degree, he did so with a certain amount of trepidation. He had the points and, having performed reasonably well in the science modules at his state exams, convinced himself that science was the road to travel. But now this decision was unravelling in front of his eyes.

He knew how hard his parents had worked to assist him in attending college. Michael was ashamed at what they and others at home would think of him if they learned of his current tribulations. There was of course the option of switching courses. But he kept delaying this decision by not revealing to his parents or college authorities his deep unhappiness with his current course.

His mood suffered, and he drank heavily to numb his pain and distress. Michael began to miss classes and tutorials, spending increasing periods of time in his room, sometimes in bed. He invented excuses as to why he was not visiting home more often and even shut down his current relationship. As his mood dropped further, thoughts of self-harm became stronger. He felt completely trapped, unable to see a path out of the mess he had created courtesy of his original poor decision. He checked out the relevant sites and they made it look so easy. Luckily, before matters came to a crisis point, his mother suddenly arrived to check on him. She sensed that something was not right and came to see for herself.

She coaxed Michael into a full disclosure as to how depressed he had become and how guilty he felt about making the wrong decision in relation to college. His mum realised that he had slipped into a bout of significant depression because of this decision and was going to require some professional assistance.

Michael attended the college GP and counselling services with her. The former agreed that the stress of his situation had triggered a bout of depression and initiated a course of medication together with some lifestyle changes such as giving up alcohol and exercising more. He also suggested referring him to see a colleague, Dr Jim, when his mood began to lift.

Michael agreed with this course of action and to take time off his course on medical grounds. His mother also commented that Michael had in her opinion always suffered from low self-esteem and was hopeful that Dr Jim might be able to assist him to increase this.

Six weeks later, Michael is feeling better and his mood has risen. He is less fatigued, and his memory and concentration are improving. He attends Dr Jim, who agrees with his college GP that the stress of the situation had triggered a bout of clinical depression and is pleased that the medication and exercise regimen are taking effect.

Michael explains the sequence of events that had led him to Dr Jim's door, including his thoughts of self-harm, and his mother and college counsellor's concerns about his low self-esteem. Dr Jim empathises and suggests using CBT techniques to explore his thinking and behaviours. He tells Michael about rational and irrational beliefs and lays out the ABC concepts, explaining how they will employ this system to locate and manage his irrational beliefs. They decide to use as the trigger his realisation that he had taken the wrong college course.

They initially explore the negative emotions that this decision had triggered. 'I felt initially very guilty,' Michael explains, 'later ashamed and then depressed.'

'So now we have the trigger and the negative emotions it created,' says Dr Jim. They decide to place these emotions in order of importance.

'I think the major one was depression,' answers Michael, 'then shame and to a lesser extent guilt.'

Dr Jim agrees and asks Michael, 'What was it about the realisation that you were on the wrong course that made you feel depressed?'

Michael finds this easy to answer.

'I was so stupid to have made this mistake. If I had done more research on the subject, I would have picked something more suitable. I also thought that it confirmed all the negative stuff I have always believed about myself, that I am a failure and at times useless, even worthless!'

'And what was it about your choice that made you feel ashamed?' asks Dr Jim.

'I was dreading that my parents and siblings and friends at home would learn of my stupidity in picking the wrong course,' he replies.

'But why would their discovering this information have bothered you?' asks Dr Jim.

Michael reflects on this.

'I think they would have been very critical of me if they heard,' he replies.

'In what way would they be critical?' asks Dr Jim.

'I assume they would end up making some judgements about me,' he replies, 'that I was stupid and a failure. Or that I wasn't strong enough to just suck it up and finish the course I had chosen.'

'And what was it about the choice you made that made you feel guilty?' asks Dr Jim.

Michael replies that he knew his parents were making significant sacrifices to put him through college and how he was wasting their hard-won financial reserves with his stupidity.

They move on to his behaviours when depressed. Michael reveals how he had isolated himself, spending a lot of time in bed. He missed lectures, withdrew socially, began drinking heavily and considered self-harm. He also couldn't get out of his own head. 'The negative thoughts went around and around my mind,' he admits. 'I just could not turn them off.' In relation to his shame and guilt, Michael notes that he reduced and almost ceased visits home as he was unable to face his family.

They add this information to Michael's ABC:

A – Activating Event:
- Trigger: taking wrong college course
- Inference/danger: he didn't do enough research before making decision; that his poor decision meant that he was stupid and a failure; that he was weak as he was unable to continue on and finish the course (even if the wrong one); that his parents, family and friends would judge him as weak and a failure and stupid if they found out about his mistake; that he had ended up wasting his parents' hard work and financial reserves because of his bad decision

B – Belief/Demands:

C – Consequences:
- Emotional reactions: depression; shame and guilt
- Physical reactions: fatigue and sleep difficulties; difficulties with concentration and memory

- Behaviour: rumination; isolating himself in his room and socially; spending too much time in bed; ceasing exercise; eating poorly; missing lectures; drinking more; considering self-harm; avoiding trips home to see his family

'So now let's examine what irrational beliefs were triggered by this situation and the inferences you assigned to it,' says Dr Jim. 'This usually takes the form of some absolute demands you are making about the trigger.'

With Dr Jim's help, Michael identifies that the irrational belief in relation to feeling depressed about his bad choice was that 'because he had made this poor decision, he was stupid, a failure, useless, worthless and weak'. In relation to Michael's emotion of shame, his irrational belief and demand was that 'people if they discover his secret (poor decision), will judge him accordingly and that he must accept their judgement'. Finally, in relation to his emotion of guilt that 'Michael should have known that this was the wrong decision and should not have made it'.

They add this information to complete Michael's ABC:

A – Activating Event:
- Trigger: taking wrong college course
- Inference/danger: he didn't do enough research before making decision; that his decision meant that he was stupid and a failure; that he was weak as he was unable to continue on and finish the course, even if the wrong one; that his parents, family and friends would judge him as weak and a failure and stupid if they found out about his mistake; that he had ended up wasting his parents' hard work and financial reserves because of his bad decision

B – Belief/Demands: 'Because I chose the wrong course, I am stupid, useless, a failure, worthless and weak.' 'People will discover that I have made this decision and judge me. I must accept their judgement.' 'I should have known the decision I made would turn out to be wrong and should not have made it.'

C – Consequences:

- Emotional reactions: depression; shame and guilt
- Physical reactions: fatigue and sleep difficulties; difficulties with concentration and memory
- Behaviour: rumination; isolating himself in his room and socially; spending too much time in bed; ceasing exercise; eating poorly; missing lectures; drinking more; considering self-harm; avoiding trips home to see his family

Dr Jim then explores with Michael how his behaviours had worsened his difficulties. How isolating himself away from parents, family, friends and his course had only increased his emotions of depression and shame. And how procrastinating in relation to dealing with the matter had allowed it to grow legs in his mind. Michael also agrees to focus more on lifestyle changes to do with his diet and exercise, cease alcohol for the present and join a college self-help group.

'Let's now examine and challenge your "B", or your irrational beliefs,' says Dr Jim. 'We are going to firstly challenge your belief "that you were stupid, useless, worthless, a failure and so on". Is this belief rational or irrational?' he inquires.

Michael replies that to him this seemed eminently rational.

'Am I not stupid and a failure for making such a bad decision?' he queries. 'Is this not only a reflection of what I have often though about myself? That my self-esteem is low?'

'But can you tell me what self-esteem is?' asks Dr Jim.

'Is it not about how we value or think about ourselves?' replies Michael, confused by the question.

Dr Jim asks him: 'Can you put a value or measurement on a human being? Is there a scale we can use?'

'Is it not about how much we are worth?' replies Michael.

'Would that be in euros, sterling or dollars?' asks Dr Jim with a smile.

Michael begins to see what Dr Jim is doing.

'What you are saying is that we cannot put a value on a human being,' he suggests, and Dr Jim agrees.

'We are not commodities, to be measured or weighed in such a manner,' he elaborates. 'What you are doing in practice is playing what we call the rating game.'

Michael is intrigued.

Dr Jim then performs the Rating Exercise detailed earlier, with Michael noting how quickly his rating dropped when Dr Jim asks him about his personal rating on discovering how he made the wrong choice of course. And how he assumed others' rating of him would also plummet because of this decision.

After some further in-depth discussion, they both agree that there are no criteria to rate a human being.

'So, this exercise is a trap?' Michael queries. Dr Jim agrees. 'But it is one so many of us fall into,' he adds.

Dr Jim introduces the concept of unconditional self-acceptance. This leads to a long discussion on Ellis's insights and how much Michael would benefit from absorbing his messages.

'This will also assist you in ceasing to accept that others have the power to judge you,' Dr Jim adds. 'The only difference between the thinking behind depression and shame is that in the first case you believe that "you" are useless, a failure and so on; and in the latter scenario that you believe that "others" think the same of you and you "must agree" with their opinions.'

This is a light-bulb moment for Michael and one that would change his life.

Dr Jim explains that Michael's difficulties have little to do with self-esteem (which both agree is a false belief or myth) and all to do with his tendency to constantly rate himself and allowing others to do so whilst accepting their judgement. They discuss the PC and how it was trying to bully Michael into believing he was a 'failure' or 'weak' or 'useless'. Michael quickly identifies this critical inner voice and how it had been present since his early teens. He vows to challenge the bully.

Michael agrees to carry out the Unconditional Self-acceptance exercise detailed earlier for the following three months. Dr Jim demonstrates how to challenge the PC on paper and Michael is relieved to discover that he is not a 'failure' but had simply failed at his task of making the right choice for college, which was a decision and thus a behaviour. He also becomes quite determined 'to get back on his feet and try again'.

Over the new few months Michael finds himself regularly grappling on paper with his PC, especially when the latter tried to make him believe he was 'worthless'. But as Dr Jim had explored with him, if he was 'worth less', then someone else was 'worth more'. But since there was no scale to measure the 'worth' of a human being, such beliefs are meaningless. Michael learns to also challenge on paper his behaviour and skills in different situations and decide on how to improve on them if required.

Three months later, he reports to Dr Jim how he is winning the battle with his PC. His inner critical voice is gradually being silenced. His mood has by now greatly improved. With Dr Jim's and his GP's assistance, and with agreement from his parents, he has plotted out a route with the college as to how to change courses. He has started a part-time job to help defray some of the costs involved. Dr Jim has also assisted him to banish his guilt in relation to his decision: did he have the 'sight' or ability to see into the future when he was making his decision? Michael realises that in life we all make decisions, of which some will work and others not, and we must live with this reality.

Nine months later, Michael was off medication and happily immersed in his new course. He had become a mental-health champion in the college, running a self-help group, and was regularly on social media encouraging those feeling down or suicidal to contact him or to ring the relevant helplines. He also regularly debunked the self-esteem myth with his peers, introducing them instead to Ellis's insights at every opportunity. He was now an Ambassador for the Unconditional Self-acceptance movement!

8. UNCONDITIONAL SELF-ACCEPTANCE AND RELATIONSHIPS

Why Relationships?

In earlier chapters we challenged the myth that success or failure in interpersonal relationships depended on whether we had low or high self-esteem. This does not exclude interpersonal relationships from being one of the most powerful triggers for self- and other-rating. We can all relate to powerful negative emotions such as anxiety, depression and on occasions shame or hurt, triggered by difficulties created in this important domain of our lives. I am going to focus on personal rather than other relationships as this is where the most significant issues arise.

Why is this the case? Personal relationships matter deeply to us all. We tend to rate ourselves positively or negatively depending on whether such relationships are running smoothly or not. If relationships break up, we can be extremely self-critical of ourselves as human beings (and on occasions of the other party in the relationship or of others we subsequently meet) rather than accepting that it is 'relationships' that fail, 'not us as human beings'!

At the heart of such difficulties lies the absence of unconditional self-acceptance. We are playing the rating game. If things are going well, we rate ourselves upwards, and if badly, downwards. This explains why so many of us become emotionally anxious, depressed, jealous and especially hurt when problems occur. There is a powerful link between our mental health and relationship difficulties. I have seen such issues trigger severe bouts of clinical depression, self-harm attempts, misuse and abuse of substances and intense bouts of anxiety.

Many of you reading this section will empathise with the intense negative emotions detailed above. Some will recognise how their mental health was impacted by the ensuing mental-health challenges.

The challenges

There are many interpersonal situations that have the potential to challenge us and trigger self- and other-rating.

Typical examples include:

1. Relationship break-ups (either short-term but especially long-term ones).
2. Relationship conflicts, either interpersonal or secondary to family issues.
3. Where one side is more 'interested' than the other in a long-term relationship.
4. When one is struggling to find a long-term partner.
5. Where one believes other people's relationships are more interesting, creative and dynamic than one's own.
6. Where one feels that the balance of the relationship is skewed, or one side believes that they are not being validated.
7. Where one has unrealistic expectations of their interpersonal relationship.

In all these situations, difficulties arise when we rate ourselves depending on whether we can resolve the issues to our satisfaction or not. It is often this personal self-rating that leads to the mental-health challenges outlined.

Unconditional Self-acceptance and Relationships

So many of us become frozen in our lives when relationship difficulties occur, and we can powerfully personally self-rate. The PC is often triggered into action, lambasting us at every possible occasion and triggering us to play the rating game with others, as in hurt. This can have devastating effects on our mental health, but also on our capacity to develop meaningful, nurturing long-term relationships.

If you could replace this tendency with unconditional self-acceptance and learn to accept and forgive yourself and others as the wonderfully unique individuals you are and shift the conversation in your heads to your own and others' behavioural responsibilities, much would change. The benefits which would accrue would be immense. Your mental health would be transformed and protected, and present and future relationships nurtured and sheltered.

Unconditional self-acceptance has the power to revolutionise your life in this area.

Let's meet some people who have come to understand its importance.

Sarah's story

Sarah is twenty-eight and attends Dr Jim with a history of anxiety and low mood. She had just broken up with her most recent boyfriend and this triggered her to seek his assistance. Coming from a rural area, she has been living in the city for five years, working as an assistant to a city banker. Despite years of the 'dating game' and numerous short-term relationships, she had so far been unlucky in her search to meet the 'right' person. She was a perfectionist and whilst this trait was seen by her boss as a plus, it was less than helpful in her quest to find the man of her dreams! She also admitted to being embarrassed when talking to her peers or family members when the subject of relationships came up.

Sarah lays out her problems to Dr Jim and queries if her self-esteem is low. She wonders if this was the cause of her current difficulties in finding the right partner and her issues with low mood and anxiety. Could he demonstrate some techniques as to how she could boost it?

Dr Jim empathises with her difficulties and suggests using some CBT techniques to deal with them. He tells Sarah about rational and irrational beliefs and lays out the ABC concepts, explaining how they will employ this system to locate and manage her irrational beliefs. They use as a trigger her recent relationship break-up.

'How did this break-up make you feel?' begins Dr Jim.

Sarah explains that she became 'anxious and depressed' following her boyfriend's decision to finish the relationship. 'I also was ashamed of what my family and friends would think when they heard of yet another failure on the romantic front,' she adds ruefully!

They decide that her main negative emotion was anxiety, followed closely by depression and shame.

'How did you feel physically, Sarah, when you became anxious?' asks Dr Jim. She admits to fatigue, tension headaches, stomach in knots, difficulties with sleep and struggling with concentration at work.

'And what did you do on becoming anxious?' he queries.

Sarah admits to catastrophising about the future, seeking reassurance from her closest friend (the one person she could share her worries with) and being constantly on her social-media and dating sites. She also reveals that when her mood fell, she began to isolate herself and lost her appetite.

They add this information to Sarah's ABC:

A – Activating Event:
- Trigger: recent break-up from boyfriend
- Inference/danger:

B – Belief/Demands:

C – Consequences:
- Emotional reactions: anxiety; depression and shame
- Physical reactions: stomach is in knots; muscle tension; sleep difficulties; tension headaches; fatigue
- Behaviour: catastrophising; seeking reassurance from best friend; stopped eating; constantly checking her social-media and dating sites

'So, what was it about this break-up that was making you feel anxious?' asks Dr Jim. 'What danger were you attributing to it?'

Sarah explains that her first thought was: 'Here we go again – another failure!'

'But why would that make you anxious?' asks Dr Jim.

'Because it has happened so many times before,' she explains. 'I am so excited when I begin a new relationship, always hoping that "this will be the one" but then after a while I notice all the little imperfections in the person and begin to pull back. They in turn assume that I am no longer interested and break off the relationship.'

They both agree that this pattern was related to her perfectionism and Dr Jim promises to return to this issue later.

'But what is your real danger?' he asks Sarah.

'That I will never find someone to be with,' she replies with tears in her eyes. 'I can see it already, alone and lonely with everyone pitying me,' she adds.

'And what is it about the break-up that made you feel depressed?' he asks.

'I just believed that I was a failure and useless,' Sarah answers. 'All my friends are settled in long-term relationships, some with children by now,' she added.

They agree that it was 'what would they think of her on hearing that she is still on her own' that was fuelling her shame.

'So now let's examine what irrational belief was triggered by the break-up and the danger you assigned to it that was making you feel anxious,' says Dr Jim. 'This usually takes the form of some absolute demand you are making about the trigger.'

Sarah, with Dr Jim's assistance, identified that her main demands were that 'she must not end up alone and lonely, if this happens, she is a failure for letting it happen' and 'she must find the perfect partner, if not, she is a failure'.

'And what irrational belief was triggered by the break-up that led to feeling depressed?' Dr Jim asks.

After some reflection, Sarah decided that it was that 'because her boyfriend left her, and she was struggling to find a partner, she was a failure'.

They agree that her demand in relation to her emotion of shame was that 'she must accept the negative judgement of others in relation to her current romantic travails'.

They add this information to Sarah's ABC:

A – Activating Event:
- Trigger: recent break-up from boyfriend
- Inference/danger: that this break-up was part of a pattern due to her desire to find the perfect partner; that she was destined to repeat this pattern and end up alone and lonely; if this happened, she would be a failure and others would end up pitying her. That because her boyfriend had left her and was struggling to find a partner, she was a failure

B – Belief/Demands: 'I must not be left alone and lonely – if this happens, I am a failure.' 'I must find the perfect partner – if not, I am a failure.' 'Because my boyfriend left me, I am a failure.' 'Others will judge me, and I must not accept their judgement.'

C – Consequences:
- Emotional reactions: anxiety; depression and shame
- Physical reactions: stomach is in knots; muscle tension; sleep difficulties; tension headaches; fatigue
- Behaviour: catastrophising; seeking reassurance from best friend; stopped eating; constantly checking her social-media and dating sites

Dr Jim then challenges Sarah's thinking and behaviour.

They agree that her unhealthy behaviours were not assisting her in finding a suitable soulmate and were contributing to her emotions of anxiety and depression. She agrees to work with him to try to change them. He promises to return later to assist her in dealing with her perfectionism.

'Let's now examine and challenge your "B", or your irrational belief,' says Dr Jim. 'This took the form of an absolute demand that you must not be left alone and lonely, and must find the perfect partner: if not, you are a failure. Is this demand rational or irrational?' he inquires.

After lengthy discussion, Sarah agrees that it was probably irrational, and he then asks, 'What would be a healthier demand?'

On reflection, Sarah agrees that a more rational or healthier demand might be that she would prefer if she was not left alone and lonely, but that this was out of her control as it was an impossible demand to achieve in real life.

Dr Jim explains that when we are seeking control, one of the four things we are looking for is 100 per cent certainty. Another is 100 per cent perfection, order and security.

'So, what were you looking for here?' asks Dr Jim.

'I was seeking 100 per cent certainty and especially 100 per cent perfection,' Sarah replies.

Following discussion, she accepts how it is unrealistic to demand 100 per cent certainty about this or indeed anything in life. To challenge this demand, Dr Jim suggests that over the course of the next month, she performs the coin exercise already detailed.

Sarah was taken by the understanding that every time we enter a relationship there is – like the two sides of a coin – a 50/50 chance that it might work and an equal chance that it might not, and that is life!

'But what about 100 per cent perfection?' asks Dr Jim. 'Is this truly possible in real life?'

This leads to a frank conversation as to the irrationality of this demand.

'In real life,' he explains, 'absolute perfection is impossible for any of us to achieve. There will always be some imperfections – however small.' He also explains how those of us seeking total perfection often seek out only imperfections in the world around us.

'Let's explore why this demand is causing you so much difficulties in your current quest,' says Dr Jim. 'Is it possible in real life to find any human being who is perfect?'

This leads to a discussion about how – by seeking only imperfections in each partner she encountered – she was putting the relationship in question under too much pressure. It was this behaviour that was alienating potential boyfriends from persisting.

Sarah begins to realise that it was this demand that had been destroying her chances of meeting a long-term partner and vowed to change her thinking and behaviour. To assist her, Dr Jim gives her the perfectionism exercise already detailed, where she would create and live with small daily imperfections and learn to adapt to them.

Dr Jim's next objective is to assist her to challenge the belief that 'she was a failure'. He does the Rating Exercise with her, with Sarah rating herself up and down the scale depending on what scenario was put in front of her. She realises how she had been spending her life playing this rating game. Dr Jim introduces her to the PC and how it tried to convince us when anxious or down that we are 'a failure' or 'useless' or 'worthless'. Sarah could really relate to this voice and vowed to silence the bully!

Dr Jim explains that the real secret of life is to develop unconditional self-acceptance and gives her the Unconditional Self-acceptance exercise to carry out for the following three months. He shows her how to challenge the PC on paper and she quickly understands that she 'cannot be a failure as a person but can fail at a task such as finding a partner'. She is especially buoyed by the maxim that 'the only failure in life was not getting back up again' and vows she would persist in her task no matter what. She is also very taken by the understanding that 'relationships fail – not people'.

Three months later, Sarah is in a new space. She is no longer demanding 100 per cent perfection in any area of her life. She was now in a new relationship, with Ian, and no longer demanding that he too should be 100 per cent perfect. She accepts that Ian is a normal human being, like herself, and ceases seeking out his imperfections. Instead, she seeks out his positive attributes and this is bringing them closer. She accepts that there is still a 50 per cent chance that it might or might not work out, which has removed a lot of her anxiety, but that's life!

Most of all, Sarah is now accepting herself as the special, unique human being that she is but taking responsibility for her behaviour. If she found herself relapsing, she revisited the Unconditional Self-acceptance exercise for a further month. She has learned to bin any further discussion about low self-esteem, understanding that this was simply an unhelpful myth. A year later, now that she is truly comfortable in her own skin, Sara and Ian are busy making long-term plans together!

Seamus's story

Seamus, a twenty-one-year-old undergraduate student, is referred to see Dr Jim following a serious episode of self-harm triggered by the ending of his relationship with teenage sweetheart Mary. They had been together for the previous five years. Mary had given no warning that she was unhappy in the relationship but suddenly chose to finish it. She no longer felt the same about their relationship, stressing that it had nothing to do with Seamus, but that she no longer had the same feelings for him. The break-up had a devastating effect on Seamus, whose mood began to fall. He isolated himself from family and friends and drank heavily to cope with his loss. He eventually imploded and, following a heavy drinking session, attempted to take his own life. Fate, in the form of a fellow student, intervened and, following a period in hospital, Seamus was referred to the college GP. He felt that Seamus's low mood and suicide attempt were due to a combination of his relationship break-up and heavy drinking. On his advice, Seamus attends Dr Jim, to deal with some of his issues.

He breaks down in front of Dr Jim, who listens empathetically to his story. Seamus by then is completely off alcohol and on his doctor's advice exercising daily. His mood has improved but he is still struggling to deal with his recent break-up. He mentions that his self-esteem is very low and wonders if this is why Mary left him.

Dr Jim offers to assist Seamus to deal with these issues, using some CBT techniques. He explains to Seamus about rational and irrational beliefs and lays out the ABC concepts and how they will employ this system to locate and manage his irrational beliefs. They use his recent relationship break-up as the trigger.

'How did this make you feel emotionally?' asks Dr Jim.

'I felt really depressed,' Seamus replies. 'Not hurt, just really down.'

'And how did this make you feel physically?'

'Tired and apathetic,' he replies, 'and struggling to concentrate or focus on anything.'

'And what did you do when you felt depressed?' asks Dr Jim. 'What was your behaviour?'

Seamus admits to having drunk heavily to blot out the pain, 'but this made me feel even worse the following day'. He also reveals that he began to withdraw from friends, spending more time alone in his room. 'I just didn't want to meet or talk to anyone. I also struggled to sleep, constantly going over and over in my mind what I could have done to prevent Mary leaving,' he adds. He also admits to following Mary on her social-media sites, checking if she was going out with anyone else. His diet deteriorated and he skipped lectures, even ceasing his normal exercise regimen. 'I just had no interest in anything. Eventually, I began to check out self-harm sites and tried to end it all. Even that didn't work out so well, I am such a failure,' he adds wryly.

They add this information to Seamus's ABC:

A – Activating Event:
- Trigger: recent break-up with Mary
- Inference/danger:

B – Belief/Demands:

C – Consequences:
- Emotional reactions: depression
- Physical reactions: fatigue; lack of motivation; poor concentration
- Behaviour: excess alcohol; withdrawal from friends; isolating himself in room; ruminating; constantly checking social media to see what Mary was doing; missed lectures; self-harm sites and suicide attempt

Dr Jim then asks Seamus: 'What was it about Mary ending the relationship that made you feel depressed?'

'It only confirmed what I had often believed about myself,' he replies, 'that I was a failure. I could see why she would choose to leave me. I was also struggling to visualise a life without her. We would often discuss plans. Now those plans were in ashes. I also believed I was worthless, of no value to myself or anyone else.'

'So now let's examine what irrational belief was triggered by the break-up,' says Dr Jim. 'This usually takes the form of some irrational belief or absolute demand you are making about the trigger which in this case related to your break-up with Mary.'

After some discussion, Seamus decides that because Mary had ended the relationship with him, 'he was a failure'. He also admits that he was 'useless' and 'worthless'. Dr Jim explains that it was these beliefs that had triggered his emotion of depression.

They added this information to Seamus's ABC:

A – Activating Event:
- Trigger: recent break-up with Mary
- Inference/danger: that Mary was right to end the relationship as he was a failure, useless and worthless; of no value to himself or others; struggled to visualise a future without her; that their plans for such a future were now in ashes

B – Belief/Demands: 'Because Mary decided to end the relationship, I am a failure, useless and worthless.'

C – Consequences:
- Emotional reactions: depression
- Physical reactions: fatigue; lack of motivation; poor concentration
- Behaviour: excess alcohol; withdrawal from friends; isolating himself in room; ruminating; constantly checking social media to see what Mary was doing; missed lectures; self-harm sites and suicide attempt

Dr Jim then challenges Seamus's thinking and behaviour.

They agree that his unhealthy behaviours are not helping him to manage the situation and are contributing to his depression. How could isolating himself, constantly ruminating over the ending of the relationship, drinking excessively and finally self-harming help him cope with the natural sense of loss and grief that comes with the ending of any relationship? Seamus agrees that such behaviours had indeed created further difficulties for himself and vows to tackle them further.

'Let's now examine and challenge your "B", or your irrational belief,' says Dr Jim. 'This took the form of an irrational belief that because Mary decided to end the relationship that you are a failure, useless and worthless. 'Is this belief rational?' he inquires.

Seamus really struggles with challenging this belief. 'Is it not completely rational?' he protests. 'Am I not a failure and of little value to myself or indeed anyone else?' He adds that this was something he had believed about himself during his teenage years. 'With Mary around, I had come to believe that maybe I wasn't such a failure after all,' he adds. 'But when she left, the thoughts came flooding back.' He explains that Mary had finally seen through him and this explains why she left. 'I always had low self-esteem,' he adds. 'I believe this was the real reason she left. She required someone much stronger than me in her life.'

Dr Jim persists. 'But is the belief that you are a failure, worthless or indeed weak a rational belief? Can a human being be described or measured in such terms?'

Seamus admits that he has never really thought much about these terms and what they mean in real life.

'I think it is time to do the Rating Exercise,' says Dr Jim.

Seamus performs the Rating Exercise and finds himself at the lower end of the rating scale, reduced further when asked about the effects of the relationship break-up and other scenarios. He also assumes others would be busy rating himself downwards.

'This is what I have always done,' he explains to Dr Jim.

Dr Jim then introduces him to the PC and how it tried to convince us when we are anxious or down that we are 'a failure' or 'weak' or 'worthless'. Seamus can really relate to this. 'His voice has been running my life for a long time,' he admits sadly.

This leads to a fruitful discussion on Ellis's insights. How human beings cannot be rated or described in such terms as each one is unique and special in themselves and how we all must take responsibility for our behaviour. Seamus is deeply affected by these insights.

Dr Jim explains that the real secret of life is to develop unconditional self-acceptance and gives Seamus the Unconditional Self-acceptance exercise to carry out for the following three months. He shows him how to challenge his PC on paper. Seamus realises that he was not a 'failure' as a person but has simply failed at his task of holding on to Mary in his previous relationship.

'So, what you are saying,' says Seamus, 'is that I failed in my task of holding on to this relationship with Mary at this moment in time but I am not a failure as a person.'

Dr Jim agrees but adds: 'Remember the sting in the tail. The only failure in life is not getting back up again.'

Dr Jim notes that in his experience many people change dramatically from an emotional and developmental perspective between eighteen and twenty-two and what they seek in a relationship can change overnight. 'I commonly see relationships which start in the mid- to late-teens break up in the early twenties for this reason,' he explains.

Suddenly Seamus feels a huge weight lifted off his shoulders. He is not a failure or useless. Rather, he had done his best in the relationship but for reasons other than himself, Mary had decided to end it. It was the relationship which had failed, not him! It was up to him now to seek out a new one.

But the real revelation comes when Dr Jim challenges the belief that he was 'worthless' on paper. Seamus had always believed this about himself, equating worthlessness with his 'low self-esteem' issues. However, after five minutes of attempting to define what it was, he finally admits to Dr Jim that he is struggling to do so. He now understands that a human being cannot be described or measured in such a manner. He is especially taken by the concept that if he was 'worth less', then someone else must be 'worth more'. 'Even to me' he admits, 'that sounds nuts!'

Dr Jim agrees. 'Human beings are far too special and wonderfully unique to be boxed in and described in such terms, never mind measured,' he explains.

This leads to a discussion on 'self-esteem' and how it is a mythical concept, a delusion, a false belief that we cling on to, no matter what. Seamus realises that he had fallen into the trap of thinking it was he who was the problem rather than his behaviour or skills. As he admits to Dr Jim, 'I was simply playing the rating game.' It is such a relief to know that his issues had nothing to do with self-esteem, the concept of which he consigned to the rubbish bin.

Six months later, Seamus had turned his life around. He had diligently worked on his Unconditional Self-acceptance exercise and was increasingly comfortable in his own skin. Of greater importance, he had met the new love of his life, Sally. He was now more realistic. Like all relationships, it might or might not work out. But no matter what the outcome would be, never again would he regard himself as a 'failure'.

Julie's story

Julie attends Dr Jim on the advice of her family doctor. She is fifty-five and really struggling with bouts of anxiety, low mood and occasionally shame. It has much to do with difficulties in her relationship. She was married to Tom for twenty-five years and had two children, now attending college. As the years passed, due to a combination of work pressures, children and Julie looking after her mother with dementia, they began to drift apart. Then the menopause arrived and Julie felt less attractive and piled on weight. She became increasingly anxious that Tom might decide to leave her due to an increasing number of rows and disagreements created by intimacy difficulties on top of other pressures.

Her mood dropped and she found herself increasingly isolated, spending hours aimlessly trawling through her social-media, online-shopping and chat-room sites. In her mind, everyone else's lives and relationships were more interesting and exciting than hers. She also felt her self-esteem was very low. 'I feel of little value to anyone,' as she explains to Dr Jim.

He listens to her story and empathises, noting that this could be a difficult phase, when the pressures of life can place significant strains on relationships. 'But sometimes it is not what happens to us in life that makes us distressed,' he adds, 'but how we interpret it.'

Julie is intrigued by this statement, so Dr Jim suggests that they use some CBT techniques to deal with her issues. He explains to her about rational and irrational beliefs and lays out the ABC concepts, explaining how they will employ this system to locate and manage her irrational beliefs. They use her relationship difficulties with Tom as the trigger.

'How do these difficulties make you feel emotionally?' asks Dr Jim.

'Anxious primarily, but also at other times depressed and ashamed,' she replies.

They also identify how her anxiety has been leading to persistent fatigue and tension headaches. They then discuss how Julie behaves when these emotions were triggered. How she spends time ruminating and catastrophising about the relationship. How she has been comfort and binge eating, drinking more, aimlessly trawling through social-media sites, checking Tom's phone, pulling away from friends and constantly checking her personal appearance in the mirror.

They add this information to Julie's ABC:

A – Activating Event:
  • Trigger: relationship difficulties with husband Tom
  • Inference/danger:
B – Belief/Demands:
C – Consequences:
  • Emotional reactions: anxiety; depression and shame
  • Physical reactions: fatigue; tension headaches
  • Behaviour: catastrophising; rumination; constantly trawling through her social media and other online sites; drinking more; comfort eating; isolating herself socially; checking personal appearance in mirror

'What was it about your current relationship difficulties that was making you feel anxious?' asks Dr Jim. 'What danger were you attributing to it?'

Julie admits that her main danger was that 'Tom will leave me'.

'And why would that make you anxious?' Dr Jim asks.

Julie's eyes fill with tears.

'I will be left on my own and end up lonely and bitter. I also love him to bits,' she replies.

'And what was it about these relationship difficulties that was making you feel depressed?' asks Dr Jim.

Julie replies that they were making her believe that she was a failure as she was unable to sort out the problem. She also believes that she was worthless and of little or no value to herself, husband or children.

'And ashamed?' queries Dr Jim.

Julie explains that she was ashamed that others would discover that she was having relationship difficulties and judge her accordingly.

'So now let's examine what irrational belief was triggered by your relationship difficulties and the danger you assigned to it that was making you feel anxious,' says Dr Jim. 'This usually takes the form of some absolute demand you are making about the trigger.'

Julie, with his assistance, identifies that her main demand was that 'Tom must not leave her – if this happens, she is a failure for letting it happen'.

'And what irrational belief was triggered by these relationship difficulties that led to feeling depressed?' Dr Jim asks.

Julie, following discussion, decides that it was 'because her relationship is failing, she was a failure and worthless'. They also agree that her demand in relation to her emotion of shame was that 'she must accept the negative judgement of others in relation to her current relationship difficulties'.

They add this information to Julie's ABC:

A – Activating Event:
- Trigger: relationship difficulties with husband Tom
- Inference/danger: Tom might leave her, if this happened, she might be left alone and bitter; she is a failure because her relationship is in difficulties; others might judge her if they discover she is having problems

B – Belief/Demands: 'Tom must not leave me – if he does, I am a failure.' 'I must not be left alone and bitter.' 'Because my relationship is failing, I am a failure'. 'Others will judge me, and I must accept their judgement.'

    C – Consequences:

- Emotional reactions: anxiety, depression and shame
- Physical reactions: fatigue; tension headaches
- Behaviour: catastrophising; rumination; constantly trawling through her social media and other online sites; drinking more; comfort eating; isolating herself socially; checking personal appearance in mirror

Dr Jim challenges Julie's thinking and behaviour.

They agree that the unhealthy behaviours detailed are not assisting her in achieving the objective of improving the quality of her relationship and reducing the risks of Tom leaving. And that they were contributing to her anxiety, depression and shame. She agrees to work with Dr Jim to change them.

'Let's now examine and challenge your "B", or your irrational belief,' says Dr Jim. 'This took the form of an absolute demand that Tom must not leave you and that you must not be left alone and bitter – if this happens, you are a failure. Is this demand rational or irrational?' he inquires.

Julie reluctantly agrees that it was probably irrational.

'What would be a healthier demand?' Dr Jim queries.

After discussion, Julie agrees that a more rational or healthier demand might be that 'she would prefer if Tom were not to leave her and not to be left alone and lonely but that this was out of her control'.

Dr Jim explains that when we are seeking control, we are usually seeking 100 per cent certainty. They agree that this was an impossible demand to achieve in real life. Dr Jim suggests that over the course of the next month she performs the coin exercise detailed earlier, to challenge this demand.

Dr Jim's major objective is to assist her in challenging the belief that 'she was a failure'. He does the Rating Exercise with her and Julie finds herself rating herself up and down the scale depending on what scenario was put in front of her. She begins to understand emotionally that she has been both rating herself and accepting other ratings for too long. Matters would have to change. Dr Jim then introduces her to the PC and how it tried to convince us when we are anxious or down that we are 'a failure' or 'useless' or 'worthless'. Julie could really relate to this inner dominant voice.

This leads to Dr Jim introducing Julie to Ellis's insights, which touch her deeply. 'But how can I put these ideas into practice in my life?' she asks.

Dr Jim gives her the Unconditional Self-acceptance exercise to carry out for the following three months. He shows her how to challenge the PC on paper and Julie quickly realises that she 'cannot be a failure as a person but can be failing at this moment in time in relation to some aspects of her relationship'.

This leads to a healthy discussion of what Julie can do to improve the quality of the relationship. She decides firstly to work on personal appearance, diet and exercise, which would make her feel more confident about her self-image. They also decide that a frank conversation needs to be had with Tom to explore why they have been drifting apart and what measures both could take to improve the situation. Julie also admits that she needs to take her life by the scruff of its neck and do a root-and-branch renewal.

She begins by working hard on her lifestyle and image, making changes to her diet, exercise regimen and appearance. She has always loved clothes, so decides to take a part-time job with a high-street retail unit, selling the latest fashion designs. Naturally some of the outfits find their way into her new wardrobe! She begins to look and feel twenty years younger as a result of all her endeavours. She re-establishes contact and meets up with some old friends from whom she had drifted apart. She also puts considerable effort into performing the Unconditional Self-acceptance exercise and sees it bearing much fruit.

On subsequent visits, she also reveals to Dr Jim how in a deeply emotional discussion with Tom, much was laid bare. He, too, was extremely unhappy with himself and the quality of their relationship but assumed that he was the reason that the latter was failing. He also admitted that he had been burying himself in work to block it out. Julie suggests counselling but after a lengthy discussion they agree to try to work things out between themselves. This turns out to be a sensible decision.

Over the following months, both work on the relationship and matters greatly improve in all aspects of their personal lives, including intimacy. Romantic weekends and time spent away on breaks have become embedded into their schedule and the positive effects are clearly obvious to all who know them. Friends on both sides comment on how well they are looking.

Nine months later, Julie is in a new space. She has now lost several stones in weight, rarely drinks and looks radiant. She has found new meaning in both her life and her relationship. She no longer believes that she is a failure or worthless or that she has no value as a person and has consigned the concept of self-esteem to the rubbish bin where, as she explains to Dr Jim, 'it belongs'. She and Tom have both learned to accept themselves unconditionally. Both are at last comfortable in their own skins.

9. UNCONDITIONAL SELF-ACCEPTANCE AND THE WORKPLACE

Why the Workplace?

We explored earlier the many false claims made about self-esteem and the workplace. The notion that those with high self-esteem performed better at work and were better leaders. That boosting self-esteem would improve the effectiveness of those in the workplace. And we saw how research has firmly debunked these myths.

Nevertheless, the workplace is a perfect breeding ground for the equally destructive world of self- and other-rating. Business in our modern high-tech world is built on a rating platform. This has seeped into the core of many multinational and other companies, often with devastating consequences for the individuals involved and indirectly for these companies through absenteeism and presenteeism.

Companies are becoming increasingly aware of the importance of positive mental health, but often fail to appreciate the role of rating in creating many of the issues undermining it. The astonishing statistic that 18 per cent of all absenteeism from the workplace is due to stress, anxiety and depression demonstrates just how important it is for companies to dump self-esteem and begin exploring the world of rating and its effects.

It is not just multinational companies that fall into self- and other-rating. It is rampant in the world of media, in teaching, medicine, insurance, banking and many of the service industries and large bureaucratic organisations. Some professions, like teaching, are immersed in an atmosphere of rating. Is this why teachers can become as anxious as the students they care for?

The challenges
There are many challenging potential triggers for self- and other-rating in the workplace.

These include:

1. Where employees and managers undergo constant performance assessments and rating. In large multinational companies, especially in the high-tech world, this may occur every three to four months, leading to increasing stress and anxiety for those involved.
2. Where one's promotion or bonuses depend on the ratings received.
3. Working in an environment such as schools or institutions exposed to regular inspections and ratings.
4. Where there is an atmosphere of constant internal rating and comparison of team members or individual teams.
5. Where there is an atmosphere of favouritism. Some colleagues are 'worth' more than others.
6. Where one is intimidated or bullied by either a fellow colleague, manager or supervisor. This can lead to intense negative self- and other-rating.

The consequences

Underlying difficulties arising in such situations includes emotions such as anxiety, depression, shame and, on occasions, hurt and frustration. These emotions place immense strain on our personal mental health.

There are strong links between all forms of personal self-rating and indeed other-rating in the workplace and our mental health. Many of us show evidence of toxic stress, which can lead to significantly increased risks of physical illnesses but are especially challenging to our mental health. The lay term used to describe this condition is 'burnout'.

Bouts of clinical depression can be triggered by a mixture of stress allied to intense periods of personal self-rating. This sets up a vicious loop. The more depressed we become, the more we become self-critical or ruminate, which in turn worsens our symptoms of depression. Others may comfort-eat and struggle with weight difficulties, others may become anorexic if we become constantly anxious. Still others may misuse or abuse alcohol. All forms of self- and other-rating can also lead to intense bouts of anxiety or frustration, neither of which impede positive mental health.

Unconditional Self-acceptance and the Workplace

You may see yourself in many of the situations described above or relate to some of the mental-health challenges explored. You may be convinced that your issues lie with self-esteem. If so, I strongly advise you to read back through chapter six on unconditional self-acceptance and on how to acquire it. Then progress to reading the cases below involving the workplace, where others have learned to bin self-esteem, identify where they were personally self-rating, and instead nurtured unconditional self-acceptance.

If unconditional self-acceptance was universally applied in the workplace, it could have a positive transformational and nurturing effect on the mental health of those involved. I believe that large companies who choose to highlight and promote its importance will retain key personnel, create a better working atmosphere, improve team performance and save costs in terms of absenteeism and presenteeism from the consequences of mental-health difficulties.

Let's explore how it changed the lives of three people struggling with workplace difficulties.

Luke's story

Luke, who is twenty-seven and working in a high-tech multinational company as a marketing manager, is referred to Dr Jim by his family doctor with a history of persistent anxiety, panic attacks, increasing levels of stress and occasional low mood. His GP had ruled out common causes of fatigue and believed his difficulties lay at work. He is in a long-term stable relationship with Mark and has no interpersonal issues. He had always considered himself as possessing high self-esteem and was struggling to understand his current difficulties. Things had come to a head on receiving a negative work assessment in comparison to his two most recent previous ones, which had been carried out at three-month intervals. He was accustomed to the world of success and was struggling to deal with the spectre of failure.

Dr Jim empathises with Luke's current difficulties and offers to assist him to manage them, using CBT techniques. He tells Luke about rational and irrational beliefs and lays out the ABC concepts, explaining how they will employ this system to locate and manage his irrational beliefs. They agree to use his recent negative assessment as the trigger.

'How did this make you feel emotionally?' asks Dr Jim.

'I just felt really anxious and later depressed,' Luke replies.

'And how did this make you feel physically?'

'Apart from the panic attacks, which have plagued me for so long, I felt so tired all the time,' answers Luke, 'constantly tense and wired, struggling to concentrate and my sleep was all over the place. I also had jaw pain from teeth grinding at night. And I kept running to the toilet with cramps and loose stools,' he adds.

'And what did you do when you became very anxious?' queries Dr Jim. Luke admits to seeking reassurance from his partner and work colleagues, catastrophising about losing his job, attending his GP for medical assessment of his panic episodes and fatigue, drank more and was overzealous in dealing with current projects.

They add this information to Luke's ABC:

A – Activating Event:
- Trigger: recent negative work assessment
- Inference/danger:

B – Belief/Demands:

C – Consequences:
- Emotional reactions: anxiety and depression
- Physical reactions: fatigue; poor concentration; panic symptoms; sleep difficulties; teeth grinding
- Behaviour: excess alcohol; catastrophising; seeking reassurance from partner Mark and work colleagues; visited GP; became overzealous at work

Dr Jim then asks Luke, 'What was it about this negative work assessment that made you feel anxious?'

'I believed that my job was now seriously at risk,' he replies. 'Another such assessment and they might let me go.'

'And has your boss informed you that this is the case?' enquires Dr Jim.

Luke shakes his head.

'He didn't go that far, but I could see where it was heading. I was also concerned about losing my bonuses at the end of the year,' he adds.

'And why would you be anxious if you did lose your job?' asks Dr Jim.

Luke replies that he might struggle to get such a well-paid, interesting job if he was let go.

'In fact, I might struggle to get another job in this sector at all, if my references were poor,' he adds. He explains that he and Mark might then struggle to pay their mortgage and would have to vacate their apartment. He adds that he would believe that he was a complete failure if all of this were to happen.

'So now let's examine what irrational belief was triggered by the negative assessment,' says Dr Jim. 'This usually takes the form of some irrational belief or absolute demand you are making about the trigger, which in this case related to your negative work ratings.'

Following discussion, Luke agrees that his demand was that 'he must not lose his job; if this happens, he would be a failure for letting it happen'.

They add this information to Luke's ABC:

A – Activating Event:
- Trigger: recent negative work assessment
- Inference/danger: that if he has another negative

assessment that he might lose his job; he and his partner Mark might lose their apartment; he might struggle to find a similar post, he might lose his bonuses at the end of the year; if all of this were to happen, he would be a failure

B – Belief/Demands: 'I must not lose my job or my bonuses; if I do, I am a failure for letting it happen'.

C – Consequences:

- Emotional reactions: anxiety and depression
- Physical reactions: fatigue; poor concentration; panic symptoms; sleep difficulties; teeth grinding
- Behaviour: excess alcohol; catastrophising; seeking reassurance from partner Mark and work colleagues; visited GP; became overzealous at work

Dr Jim having first assisted him to use the Flooding technique discussed on page 132 to banish his panic attacks, then challenges Luke's thinking and behaviour. They agree that his unhealthy behaviours are not assisting him in managing his current situation and are contributing to his emotions of anxiety and depression. How could catastrophising, drinking too much and constantly seeking reassurance from Mark and others, assist him in dealing with his issues? Luke vows to challenge and change them.

'Let's now examine and challenge your "B", or your irrational belief,' says Dr Jim. 'This took the form of an irrational belief that "you must not lose your job; if you do, you are a failure". Is this belief rational?' he enquires.

After protracted discussion, Luke finally agrees that it was probably irrational, and Dr Jim then asks, 'What would be a healthier demand?'

After further discussion, Luke agrees that a more rational or healthier demand might be that 'he would prefer not to lose his job, but that this was out of his control'. This led to a discussion on the importance of control.

Dr Jim explains that when we are seeking control, we are usually seeking 100 per cent certainty. Luke agrees that this was an impossible demand to achieve in real life.

Dr Jim suggests that over the course of the next month, Luke performs the coin exercise detailed earlier, to challenge this demand.

But Dr Jim was especially interested in the second irrational belief they had uncovered where Luke believed 'he was a failure'.

'Is this belief rational or irrational?' he queries.

'I think it is completely rational,' replies Luke. 'Am I not a failure if assessed negatively, as in this case?'

Dr Jim persists.

'But is the belief that you are a failure and worthless a rational belief? Can a human being be described or measured in such terms?'

This leads to a discussion on the world of rating.

Dr Jim asks Luke to perform the Rating Exercise. Unsurprisingly, he rated himself at the higher end of the scale. 'I always felt I should be the best,' he explains. He also noted that others, in his opinion, also rated him highly. However, on being asked to rate himself following his negative assessment, his rating plummeted from ninety-five to seventy-five, as did his other rating.

Dr Jim also introduces him to the PC and how it tries to convince us when we are anxious or down that we are 'a failure' or 'useless' or 'worthless'.

Luke admits that this is a voice that he could relate to, especially its snide comments about him being a 'failure'.

'I am so used to success,' he admits, 'I just can't cope if I cannot achieve the high standards that I set for myself.'

Dr Jim introduces him to Ellis's insights and Luke is initially alarmed by Ellis's tenets.

'Are you saying that I am not allowed to rate myself at all?' Luke queries.

Dr Jim agrees. This leads to a long discussion on how Luke has spent his whole life, in the world of high self-rating.

'It is going to be really difficult for me to cease doing this,' he admits. 'I have always lived for my rating. It's what gives me a buzz.'

'If it is working so well for you,' asks Dr Jim with a smile, 'why are you here?'

They have a good laugh at this comment, with Luke being forced to agree that his 'ratings' were doing him no favours. Maybe it was time to change!

Dr Jim explains that the real secret of life is to develop unconditional self-acceptance and he gives Luke the Unconditional Self-acceptance exercise to carry out for the following three months. He then shows him how to challenge his PC on paper. They have a good discussion on why Luke could not be a failure as a person but could fail at a task (such as his current assessment) at a moment in time. Nor could he be described as a 'success' if his next assessment was more positive. Human beings could not be rated in such a manner. It was quite acceptable, however, to rate his work effectiveness.

'The problems begin, Luke,' explains Dr Jim, 'when we base our assessments of ourselves as human beings on whether we are successful or not at a task or assessment.'

This was a watershed moment for Luke, who had always felt under pressure 'to deliver' so that he could consider himself a success but had always struggled if he failed to do so. It was this irrational belief that had triggered his most recent difficulties.

Over the following few months, through regularly performing the Unconditional Self-acceptance exercise, Luke noticed how he was gradually coming to accept himself 'unconditionally' and, as a result, becoming less anxious and stressed. He also sat down with his superiors and discussed how 'useful' these constant assessments were in practice and how they were creating an unhealthy workplace environment. This led to a change of approach from his employers and paradoxically to an increased output and efficiency in the teams involved.

The good news came with his subsequent assessments now spaced out at better intervals. These were extremely positive. But Luke had learned his lesson, understanding that it was the work that he had put into the projects that could be rated – not himself as a person.

Jenifer's story

Jenifer is thirty-six and a busy primary school teacher who is happily married to Joe, with two small children. She had always tended to be anxious but hid it from those around her. Then word went out that a 'difficult' school inspection had taken place at a nearby school. She started to become increasingly anxious, struggling with fatigue and sleep. On the advice of her GP, whom she attends for a check-up, Jenifer comes to see Dr Jim for some assistance.

Dr Jim listens to her current difficulties and offers to assist her using some CBT techniques. He tells her about rational and irrational beliefs and lays out the ABC concepts, explaining how they will employ this system to locate and manage his irrational beliefs.

They use the news relating to the adjoining school inspection as the trigger.

'How did this make you feel emotionally?' asks Dr Jim.

'My anxiety levels soared,' she replies.

'And how did this make you feel physically?' he asks.

Jenifer notes that she became increasingly fatigued, developed tension headaches and struggled with sleep.

'And what did you do, Jenifer?' he asks. 'What was your behaviour when you became so anxious?'

She admits to spending countless hours on her daily and weekly plans, beginning to comfort-eat, seeking reassurance from her principal, other colleagues and husband. She also spent hours catastrophising as to how awful such an inspection might be.

They add this information to Jenifer's ABC:

A – Activating Event:
- Trigger: local adjoining school has inspection
- Inference/danger:

B – Belief/Demands:

C – Consequences:
- Emotional reactions: anxiety
- Physical reactions: stomach is in knots; sleep difficulties; tension headaches; fatigue
- Behaviour: catastrophising; comfort eating; seeking reassurance from colleagues and husband; spending countless hours on her class plans

'So, what was it about hearing about the adjoining school inspection that was making you feel so anxious?' asks Dr Jim. 'What danger were you attributing to it?'

Jenifer admits that her main danger was that she would be next in line for the dreaded school inspector.

'But why would that make you anxious?' he asks.

'Because I might not be sufficiently prepared on the day, if he arrives unannounced,' she explains. She elaborated on how her daily and weekly plans would be put under the spotlight if such an inspection were to occur. 'If these were not perfect, the inspection might not go well,' she adds.

'And why would you be anxious if the inspection went badly?' asks Dr Jim.

Jenifer replies that it would reflect badly on both her and the school.

'And why would it bother you if this happened?' he asks.

'Because I would believe that I was a failure if this occurred,' she explains. 'I have always suffered from low self-esteem, so would struggle to deal with such negative feedback.'

'So now let's examine what irrational belief was triggered on hearing about the recent school inspection,' says Dr Jim. 'This usually takes the form of some absolute demand you are making about the trigger that was making you anxious.'

Jenifer, with his assistance, identifies that her main demand was 'she must do well in her inspection – if not, she is a failure'.

They add this to her ABC:

A – Activating Event:
- Trigger: local adjoining school has inspection
- Inference/danger: maybe she is going to be next in line for an inspection; that if one occurs, she might not have her daily and weekly plans sufficiently laid out; if this happens, she might fail the test and humiliate herself and her school

B – Belief/Demands: 'I must do well in any school inspection; if not, I am a failure'.

C – Consequences:

- Emotional reactions: anxiety
- Physical reactions: stomach is in knots; sleep difficulties; tension headaches; fatigue
- Behaviour: catastrophising; comfort eating; seeking reassurance from colleagues and husband; spending countless hours on her class plans

Dr Jim then challenges Jenifer's thinking and behaviour.

They agree that her behaviour, especially hours spent on excessively complex daily and weekly plans for an inspection that might not occur for years, was unhelpful. As was seeking constant reassurance from those around her.

'Let's now examine and challenge your "B", or your irrational belief,' says Dr Jim. 'This took the form of an absolute demand that "you must do well in any school inspection, if not you are a failure". Is this demand rational or irrational?' he enquires.

Jenifer reluctantly agrees that it was irrational, and Dr Jim then asks, 'What would be a healthier demand?'

After some discussion, they agree that a more rational or healthier demand might be that 'she would prefer if she did well in any upcoming school inspection, but that this was out of her control'.

Dr Jim explains that when we are seeking control, we are usually looking for 100 per cent certainty. They agree that this is an impossible demand to achieve in real life. Dr Jim suggests that over the course of the next month, Jenifer should perform the coin exercise to challenge this demand.

But he spends most of the visit focusing on Jenifer's belief that 'she is a failure' and on her misguided beliefs about self-esteem. 'Is your belief that you are a failure, rational or irrational?' he asks.

After some disputation, Jenifer reluctantly agrees that it is probably irrational. 'I still remain to be convinced!' she adds.

Dr Jim performs the Rating Exercise, with Jenifer rating herself up and down the scale depending on what scenario was put in front of her, especially the possibility that she makes a mess of her future school inspection. She rates herself quite low if it were to go badly and quite high if it goes well and assumes others would do similarly.

Dr Jim then introduces Jenifer to the PC and how it tries to convince us when anxious or down that we are 'a failure'. Jenifer is well acquainted with this voice. 'She is constantly criticising me, especially in bed at night,' she adds. Dr Jim introduces her to Ellis's insights and Jenifer is anxious to learn how to put them into practice.

Dr Jim gives her the Unconditional Self-acceptance exercise to carry out for the following three months. He also shows her how to challenge the PC on paper. Jenifer has a light-bulb moment when she realises that she cannot be rated as a failure but can and will fail at specific tasks and skills. She is also intrigued after a discussion on the delusion of self-worth, that the whole concept of self-esteem was so flawed. She now accepts that human beings cannot be rated as too special and unique.

Three months later, Jenifer's anxiety levels have plummeted, and she has learned how to accept and live with uncertainty. More importantly, she has developed unconditional self-acceptance, understanding that 'failure is part of life and does not define who she is as a human being'. She has dropped any mention of self-esteem whilst dealing with pupils and their parents, focusing more on teaching them to accept themselves as the special unique human beings they are. But also encouraging them to take responsibility for any little lapses in behaviour. She has learned how to nurture and grow her own mental health and was passing this on to others.

Her positive mental health is finally tested when, a year later, an inspector does indeed arrive unexpectedly at the school to review her work. As expected, she is initially anxious but copes much better than expected. When she receives a glowing, positive assessment, however, she does not fall into the trap of now assuming 'she' was a 'success'. Rather, she was just successful on this occasion in relation to this inspection!

Miriam's story

Miriam arrives to see Dr Jim, extremely distressed, concerned about her levels of anxiety and low mood following a prolonged bout of workplace stress. She was thirty-eight, in a long-term stable relationship, and working in a high-pressure, results-driven, multinational company. Due to her hard work and perfectionist traits, she was drafted in by senior management to become second in command of the most important section in the company. This had gone down badly with other members of this section. Some had harboured ambitions of being appointed to the position themselves. Her new boss resented the fact that Miriam was appointed instead of the person she had recommended. Adding to her challenges, most of the section, apart from the section manager, were male, and some had been there for many years. It was inevitable that her introduction as an 'outsider' was going to be challenging. And so it proved!

From the beginning, she found herself subtly shunned. Her manager placed extra work on her plate, assigning the most complex and time-consuming tasks. If not delivered promptly, criticism wasn't long in coming her way. Miriam was given the least favourable workstation and, on protesting, was quickly overruled.

She found herself increasingly isolated in the section and unsure of where to turn. She was both anxious and ashamed about seeking assistance from senior management. They might assume she could not cope. Eventually Miriam began to show the classical signs of toxic stress. She became exhausted, struggled with sleep, began to suffer tension headaches and became increasingly anxious emotionally and physically. She found herself fighting more with her partner, Simon. Her mood began to fall. Simon told her that she had self-esteem issues and needed professional assistance to deal with them.

Just when she believed that matters could not get worse, a male colleague, extremely jealous of her promotion, began a campaign of subtle sexual harassment. Soon the others joined in. They were extremely careful not to make it overt, but vague sexual comments and other forms of harassment became the norm. Miriam tried to bring up the subject with her manager but was treated dismissively and directed to get on with her work. If she was not coping with her new post, maybe she should consider a transfer to another section!

Eventually Miriam's mental health began to deteriorate. She became increasingly anxious and stressed until eventually the situation triggered a bout of clinical depression. She visited her family doctor, who diagnosed depression, signed her off work on medical grounds, prescribed a course of antidepressants and tried to intervene with her personnel department. Her mood began to improve but she remained distressed about what had happened and unsure of how to deal with the situation, so she was referred to see Dr Jim.

Dr Jim listens empathetically to her story, mentioning that the situation she describes is one that he commonly encounters. This

revelation has an immediate calming effect on Miriam, who realises that she is not alone in her difficulties. She mentions how her
partner and indeed her manager had both suggested that she had
low self-esteem issues and required assistance to boost it. Perhaps
Dr Jim could show her how to do so!

Dr Jim promises to return to the subject of self-esteem later and
then suggests that they might use CBT techniques to manage her
issues. He tells Miriam about rational and irrational beliefs and
lays out the ABC concepts, explaining how they will employ this
system to locate and manage her irrational beliefs.

They agree that her current situation is complex but decide that
the trigger causing her the greatest difficulty is how her manager
treats her when seeking assistance.

'And how did this make you feel emotionally?' asks Dr Jim.

After some discussion, Miriam details in order her emotions.
'I was hurt,' she answers, 'but also anxious, depressed and finally
ashamed. But it was the hurt that affected me most deeply,' she
adds.

'And what did you do when you became hurt?' asks Dr Jim.

Miriam admits that she became hypersensitive, irritable with
those around her, argued more with Simon, her partner, and
became quite short with work colleagues and on occasions even
customers.

'And what about when you became anxious and depressed?' Dr
Jim asks.

'I began to isolate myself socially, constantly replaying my
manager's comments in my head, and began to believe that maybe
I was the problem, and I tended to drink excessive amounts of
wine,' she replies. 'I also began to check other job possibilities in
case my manager suggested that the company should let me go'.
In relation to her emotion of shame, Miriam admits to avoiding

meeting colleagues from other sections, believing that they would learn how she was being treated and judge her and treat her differently.

She also admits how she has developed a host of physical symptoms such as fatigue, tension headaches, reduced drive and motivation, struggling to sleep, and has difficulties concentrating when she becomes anxious and later depressed.

They add this information to Miriam's ABC:

A – Activating Event:
- Trigger: section manager dismissing her concerns about bullying/harassment by male colleagues and excessive workload
- Inference/danger:

B – Belief/Demands:

C – Consequences:
- Emotional reactions: hurt; depression; shame and anxiety
- Physical reactions: sleep difficulties; tension headaches; struggling with sleep; concentration and memory and fatigue
- Behaviour: catastrophising; ruminating; becoming hypersensitive and irritable with work colleagues, customers and partner; avoiding meeting colleagues from different sections; isolating herself socially; drinking too much wine

'So, what was it about your manager dismissing your concerns about the behaviour of your male colleagues and your excessive workload that caused you to feel hurt?' asks Dr Jim. 'What inference were you taking from this trigger?'

'I felt so ridiculed and dismissed,' Miriam answers, 'treated like a piece of dirt on the ground. It was awful.'

'But why would that make you feel hurt?' persists Dr Jim.

'Because these concerns of mine were real,' she answers. 'I was being constantly harassed, even if it was subtle, and she was also loading excessive work on to my plate, compared to the others.'

'And why would her treating the others differently and not challenging their behaviour or increasing their workload make you feel hurt?' asks Dr Jim.

Miriam can't believe he is asking her this question.

'Is it not obvious?' she says. 'It is so blatantly unfair, and I believe that I have the right to be treated fairly, just like everyone else.'

Dr Jim then asks, 'And what was it about the situation that made you feel depressed?'

'Because it made me think badly of myself,' she replies. 'I felt so weak that I was allowing both her and indeed my work colleagues to treat me this way.'

'And anxious?' he asks.

'My main danger was that this situation would be allowed to continue,' she replies, 'with my mental health and well-being being gradually eroded and destroyed. Not to mention my self-esteem.'

'And ashamed?' Dr Jim queries.

Miriam replies that other people would see her as she saw herself – as 'weak'.

'So now let's examine what irrational beliefs were triggered by your manager's behaviour,' says Dr Jim. 'These usually take the form of some absolute demands you are making about the trigger.'

After some discussion, they agree that in relation to her hurt she was 'demanding that she must be treated fairly, by both her manager, colleagues and indeed life itself'.

'And what irrational belief was triggered by the situation with your manager and colleague that led to feeling depressed?' he asks. Miriam, on reflection, decides that it was 'because she had not prevented them from treating her so badly, she was 'weak and worthless'. They also agree that her demand in relation to her emotion of shame was that 'she must accept the negative judgement of others, that she was "weak" in relation to her handling of the current situation'.

'And what irrational belief was triggered by the situation with manager and colleague that led to feeling anxious?' he asks. They agree that her demand in this situation was that 'she must not be exposed to this situation long term and that she must not end up with mental-health sequelae because of the situation.'

They add this information to her ABC:

A – Activating Event:
- Trigger: section manager dismissing her concerns about bullying/harassment by male colleagues and excessive workload
- Inference/danger: that her manager was dismissing her concerns about excessive workload and inappropriate subtle harassment by colleagues; that she was being ridiculed; that she was being treated differently than other members of her section; that such treatment was blatantly unfair; that she was weak and worthless for allowing this to happen; that the situation would continue indefinitely, destroying her mental health

B – Belief/Demands: 'I should not be treated like this.' 'I should be treated fairly.' 'Life should be treating me fairly.' 'Because I allowed both her manager and colleagues to treat me like this, I am weak and worthless.' 'I must accept the negative judgements of others.' 'I must not be exposed to the situation long term.' 'I must not end up with long-term mental-health difficulties.'

C – Consequences:

- Emotional reactions: hurt; depression; shame and anxiety
- Physical reactions: sleep difficulties; tension headaches; struggling with sleep; concentration and memory and fatigue
- Behaviour: catastrophising; ruminating; becoming hypersensitive and irritable with work colleagues, customers and partner; avoiding meeting colleagues from different sections; isolating herself socially; drinking too much wine

Dr Jim challenges Miriam's thinking and behaviour.

They begin by exploring the negative behaviours that she had been engaging in to cope with her complex emotions. Miriam reluctantly agrees that being hypersensitive and irritable with those around her was unhealthy. As was isolating herself socially or excessively drinking. She admitted the latter had contributed to her mood falling and vowed to change her habits. They also agree that catastrophising about the future or avoiding colleagues from different sections was not improving matters.

'Let's now examine and challenge your "B", or your irrational beliefs,' says Dr Jim. 'This initially took the form of an absolute demand in relation to your emotion of hurt, that "you must be treated fairly by both others and life". Is this demand rational or irrational?' he enquires.

This produces a strong response from Miriam.

'Of course, it is completely rational to believe that one should be treated fairly,' she protests. 'Is this not a basic right for any human being, that others should treat us fairly? I cannot understand why you are asking me this question,' she adds. 'Is it not self-explanatory?'

Dr Jim then reveals that this was the commonest response he got to this question.

'Unfortunately, this belief and demand are both completely irrational,' he adds.

This leads to a long, challenging discussion on why this was so. Eventually Miriam comes around to accepting that the rational belief that 'she would prefer if she was treated fairly but "hello, life" is a more realistic statement'.

As Dr Jim explains, it would be wonderful if everyone treated us fairly and indeed if life did the same, but this is and has always been impossible to arrange. 'Life is tough and unfair and if you believe that you are going to be treated differently than the rest of humanity,' he adds, 'you will always struggle'.

Dr Jim elaborates that when we were hurt it usually means we are carrying a 'grudge' against someone or life itself. Miriam found this insight extremely helpful, especially when asked to go home, fill a rucksack with rocks and walk with them for an hour. She was then to experience the feelings of relief and lightness when the rucksack of rocks was removed. She agrees to carry out this exercise.

'Is this grudge against your manager and indeed your colleagues helping you in your life?' Dr Jim asks, and Miriam agrees it is not.

'But how can I learn how to drop this grudge?' she asks. 'It is so deeply embedded'.

Dr Jim promises to show her how to do this. 'But first, let's explore another irrational belief that was triggered by this situation, "that you are weak and worthless." Is this belief rational?' he enquires.

'But am I not weak in allowing her and the others to treat me like this? 'Miriam protests. She also admits that her belief that she is worthless is in her eyes another sign that her self-esteem is low.

To counter such views, Dr Jim asks her to perform the Rating Exercise, where, as expected, Miriam rates herself on the lower end of the scale, decreasing further when asked about her self- and other-rating when her concerns were dismissed by her manager. When Dr Jim challenges on what grounds or using what scale she was rating herself, however, the penny suddenly drops for Miriam. Human beings cannot be measured in such a manner.

Dr Jim then introduces her to the PC and how it tries to convince us when anxious or down that we are 'weak' or 'a failure' or 'worthless'. Miriam could easily really relate to this voice. Dr Jim explores Ellis's insights with Miriam, and she is excited at the prospect of putting these ideas into practice in her life.

Dr Jim gives her the Unconditional Self-acceptance exercise to carry out for the following three months. He challenges the PC on paper regarding the belief that she is 'weak' and Miriam begins to see that such self-definitions are both unhealthy and inaccurate. She is especially blown away when they challenge her belief that she is 'worthless'. Suddenly she realises that her obsession with self-esteem was in practice unhelpful and obstructing her road to mental well-being. Dr Jim warns her that it will take months of challenging the PC for her to become comfortable in her own skin.

On their next visit, Dr Jim returns to challenging the irrational belief behind her hurt. By now, she is feeling much better, mood and cognition-wise, and has discovered through the rucksack of rocks exercise that carrying such a grudge was just wearing her down. She was also working hard on her Unconditional Self-acceptance exercise. She now understood emotionally that human beings could not be rated but their behaviour or skills could.

Dr Jim then asks her, 'Did your manager mess up in relation to how she treated you?'

Miriam agrees strongly that she had.

'But can we rate or judge her as a person?' he asks.

Suddenly Miriam sees the light.

'What you are saying is that she as a human being has messed up in her behaviour, but that does not allow us to rate her as a person,' she says.

Dr Jim agrees.

'Because there is no scale to measure her either as a human being. But we are totally justified in challenging her behaviour.'

This was a watershed moment for Miriam. They agree that it would be in her interests to forgive her boss and indeed her work colleagues, while she was completely justified in rating and challenging their behaviour.

They then discuss in detail how best to challenge someone's behaviour if it was felt to be inappropriate or unfair. They focus in on how to deal with issues which arose immediately, making the person aware of why their behaviour was an issue, making it clear it was not personal but more about their behaviour, and where necessary making the person experience the consequences of their actions.

Over the following months and with the intervention of the personnel department, Miriam returned to work but not before having a frank and fruitful encounter with her boss, who now regretted her previous behaviour towards her. She admitted to feeling vulnerable when Miriam was parachuted into her division and fearful for her own future – which, she now accepted, explained but did not condone her behaviour. With the air now clear, they drew up a new policy on how best to target the subtle harassment that Miriam had been experiencing. Her boss arranged for outside bodies to visit their section, to discuss potential consequences for any colleague, male or female, if such a claim were to be upheld. Miriam and her boss then began to work more efficiently as a management team and soon her male colleagues were taking on more tasks than had been the case previously. Her boss was quick to quell any dissenting voices, mentioning the risks of demotion or potential loss of bonuses for those who made waves. Behaviour changed, and all harassment ceased. She reconnected with colleagues in other sections, no longer concerned about what they or others thought about her. The major change in Miriam's life was that she no longer played the rating game with herself or others. She had also learned to banish the myth of self-esteem and now accepted herself unconditionally. She also ceased to assume that life should be fair to herself or others. Life was just life!

10. UNCONDITIONAL SELF-ACCEPTANCE AND BODY IMAGE

Why Body Image?

Body image relates to how we think, feel and behave in relation to our physical body. It is often intimately linked to self-esteem, in a bi-directional manner. In this scenario, if your body image is poor, it is assumed that this in turn will reduce your self-esteem. On the other hand, if your self-esteem is low, then you are more likely to suffer from poor body-image issues. The corollary being, of course, that boosting self-esteem should reduce the incidence of body-image conditions and vice versa.

We have explored in the first part of this book how flawed these concepts are. Such beliefs are built on extremely shaky foundations. We have also explored how academic research has challenged self-esteem and the multiple myths that have grown up around it. This is important as eating disorders, for example, are infinitely more complex than simply attributing the cause to self-esteem. Or assuming that boosting self-esteem would reduce their incidence.

This does not mean, however, that human beings, since the beginning of historical records, have not been obsessed with the human form. Or the reality that, depending on the cultural or historical era, these obsessions have taken on many different shapes and forms. Or the stark fact that human beings love to play the rating game in relation to perceptions of their physical bodily attributes. Men, but more especially women, have always played this game.

In this unhealthy scenario, we tend therefore to compare our body-image perceptions with those around us and the wider community. If our belief is that 'our' body image does not match up, we tend to rate ourselves downwards and so can become anxious, depressed or even ashamed. None of these emotions are healthy and can lead, as we will see, to a variety of equally unhealthy behaviours.

Social Media – the Game Changer

Whilst such body image rating has been present in various forms since early times, there can be little doubt that the arrival of technology and social media has multiplied body-image problems. We could have renamed this chapter 'The Effects of Social Media on Body Image' and based the whole discussion on social media, but it's important to explore the subject more broadly.

Allied to social media is the marketing frenzy created by multinationals creating needs and wants in each one of us individually. When we combine both phenomena together, it is easy to see why there is an explosion in anxiety, self-harm, depression and eating disorders in relation to this issue.

Underlying body-image problems is the connection in our emotional minds between the 'perfect' body image and the personal self-rating that we are 'flawed' or 'a failure' or 'weird' or 'worthless' if we cannot achieve such an image. We tend to seek out only bodily imperfections, castigating ourselves harshly if any are found. This connection has nothing to do with self-esteem but more to do with our natural tendency to self- and other-rate, depending on whether we are successful or not at a moment in time in achieving the image we crave.

We then find ourselves in the perfect loop. If we are not comfortable with our body image, we play the rating game. This in turn leads to us searching for imaginary flaws in our physical appearance and trying then to change them. As we cannot win this battle, we revert to rating ourselves further and so on. This can be a deadly trap, as the families of those who have attempted self-harm or died by suicide to escape this trap because of serious eating disorders have sadly discovered. We will also be exploring this loop when discussing obesity.

It is easy to see how social media can accelerate any tendency to enter this loop. We are bombarded with pictures of the perfect male or female body shapes online. Many of these images are doctored to remove what would be normal human imperfections, a virtual versus a real image! In adolescence especially, where the tendency to rate and compare one another is a normal phase of development, social media in the form of Instagram and other sites geared to promote the 'perfect body image' can have a devastating effect on the young vulnerable mind.

Boys begin to believe from watching non-stop porn that there is a certain muscle-bound shape that girls really desire. This has led to an explosion in the use of anabolic steroids and an obsession with the gym. Girls fall into the trap that only those with size-zero waistlines and perfect faces, hair and breasts will be attractive to boys. This has led to increasing sexualisation of young girls, and relentless grooming and tweaking of photos sent out online.

The real difficulty is that both boys and girls begin to associate their self-rating with how successful or not their efforts to achieve what they perceive as the perfect body image. As a result, they become anxious, depressed, self-harm or become hopelessly entangled in the world of eating disorders.

This is exacerbated by the capacity of multinational companies – with the assistance of giant tech and social-media companies – to target each one of us individually with products to help us achieve the perfect body image. In such a campaign, adolescents are cannon fodder, as indeed are adults! Then we have the plastic-surgery industry, promising to give us what we so desperately seek – the perfect face, nose, chin, breasts or whatever else we feel is imperfect and in need of tweaking in our body shape or image. The final link in the chain is the media 'influencers' who promote through their sites what the current look 'should be' and what products one 'must' have to achieve it.

To discuss it fully, this subject would require a further book. Nor will we deal with the complex world of eating disorders, for similar reasons. Instead, we will confine our discussion to some common issues relating to body image which relate to us all.

The challenges

These include situations where:

1. We are struggling with body-image issues relating to obesity.
2. We associate our body image with self-rating.
3. Adolescents are trapped in the world of social media, body image and self- and other-rating.
4. We find ourselves – male or female – in middle years, loathing our body image and deeply unhappy as a result.

5. We are using plastic surgery to become comfortable in our own skins at any stage in our lives.
6. We find ourselves playing the body-image rating game online; a game we are destined to lose.
7. We are becoming increasingly anxious, ashamed or depressed because of flawed body-image perceptions.
8. We find ourselves like poor old Narcissus, believing that we have or should have the perfect body and image, and spend our lives compulsively feeding this unhealthy obsession.

Body Image and Mental Health

It is important to highlight the links between body image, self-rating and mental health. Three common emotions are triggered by personal self-rating secondary to body-image issues. These are anxiety, depression and shame. None of these are assisting our mental health.

There will be some people reading this section who can relate to bouts of significant anxiety in relation to perceived body-image issues. Some may be busily attempting to control life, which is of course an impossibility, so they try instead to control their body image, through diet, excessive exercise or plastic surgery. It becomes a vicious circle. The more obsessed and concerned they become about their body image, the more they personally self-rate downwards, which in turn further feeds their anxiety. This creates a behavioural response of focusing further on improving their body image, worsening the spiral. This loop can lead us down dark roads indeed.

In others, this linking together of body image and personal or other self-rating can trigger bouts of clinical depression. This allows the PC free rein to savagely criticise us at every level, including our appearance, which in turn triggers further ruminations and drops in mood. There will be some reading this section who can relate to this reality.

Self-harm can be the result of this mixing together of body image and some of the mental-health conditions discussed above. The dark world of anorexia nervosa, which we discussed earlier, is the ultimate expression of body-image and personal self-rating. This is a slow descent into hell for many of those entangled in this mesh and their families, often ending up in the destruction of the person's physical and mental health. Substance abuse can be another method of managing our body-image difficulties.

Unconditional Self-acceptance and Body Image

But what do you do if you are struggling with this combination of body-image and either personal self-rating or other-rating? How can you break free of both? This is the question that many reading this section may be asking.

The answer to this mixture of body-image difficulties and self-rating lies in the world of unconditional self-acceptance, where we learn to become truly comfortable in our own skins, both emotionally and physically. Where we learn to accept both ourselves as human beings and with the body we possess.

This does not of course rule out any efforts made in relation to our behaviour in this area. For example, if we are overweight or obese, we might need to explore our lifestyle. Or if we are falling into the plastic-surgery/botox trap of assuming that these approaches will make us more comfortable with ourselves or using steroids and excessive body-building techniques as a male to achieve the perceived perfect body image, that is something we should question. In practice, such unhealthy behavioural patterns may worsen the underlying body-image issues, as we will have to repeat them once begun. Unconditional self-acceptance can assist us to escape this trap, by learning to accept ourselves as human beings but being prepared to rate and challenge our behaviour.

Let's now meet some people who have encountered some of the above issues and learned to apply these concepts.

Jill's story

Jill is referred to Dr Jim by her family doctor following an overdose attempt triggered by a relationship break-up. She had always been a perfectionist who struggled with anxiety and occasional bouts of low mood. As a teenager, she had never been comfortable with her body and struggled with bulimia, where she binged and purged.

In her early twenties, this pattern settled but she spent countless hours on social media, comparing her physical appearances with the 'stunning' photos of others. Although physically extremely attractive, she could never see what others saw. All she could see was a limitless conveyor belt of imperfections. Nothing was right. She found faults with her nose, ears, breast size and legs, amongst others! The fact that she worked in the media only highlighted her imperfections. All she could see around her were women who were physically 'perfect'.

Her most recent relationship cracked under the strain, confirming her belief that she was 'flawed' physically. This explained in her mind why her boyfriend had left. She believed that it was 'she' who was flawed and a failure, and her mood dropped. It was this belief that triggered her overdose, following a heavy drinking bout with friends. This occurred as she had come to believe that nobody would be interested in a long-term relationship with her, unless she could iron out her multiple bodily imperfections.

Jill admits to Dr Jim how she is becoming increasingly emotionally anxious and depressed about these imperfections, constantly researching the possibility that plastic surgery might be the answer. She also wonders about her self-esteem, which she feels is low. Maybe if she could boost her self-esteem, her body-image issues might improve!

Dr Jim empathises with her story, explaining that in the new world of social media, body-image difficulties are inevitable in our society. He then suggests that they might use some CBT techniques to deal with her issues. He tells Jill about rational and irrational beliefs and lays out the ABC concepts, explaining how they will employ this system to locate and manage her irrational beliefs. They decide to use the recent break-up from her boyfriend as the trigger.

'How did this make you feel emotionally?' Dr Jim asks.

Jill replies that she felt 'initially depressed and then extremely anxious'.

'And what was your behaviour when you felt depressed?'

Jill notes that she had begun to isolate herself more, or that she was binge-drinking socially, and she couldn't get the thoughts of how ugly she was out of her head, especially at night.

'And then I tried to end it,' she adds with tears in her eyes. 'I feel so ashamed of my actions and how much they upset my mum and sister.'

'And later, when you recovered, what did you do when you reverted back to being anxious?' Dr Jim enquires.

Jill admits to spending hours checking out her physical appearance, seeking out imperfections, which were easy to find.

'I also tweaked any pictures going out on my social-media platforms, sometimes spending hours doing so,' she adds. She also admits checking out numerous plastic surgery options to deal with her many imperfections. Jill also reveals that she spent time catastrophising about the bleak future ahead of her as 'no man will want to be around me – as I am so ugly'.

'And how did you feel physically when you were depressed and anxious?' asks Dr Jim.

Jill reports having significant fatigue, bowel problems, muscle tension and sleep difficulties.

They add this information to Jill's ABC:

A – Activating Event:
  - Trigger: recent break-up with boyfriend
  - Inference/danger:
B – Belief/Demands:
C – Consequences:
  - Emotional reactions: depression and anxiety
  - Physical reactions: stomach is in knots; muscle tension; sleep difficulties; fatigue
  - Behaviour: catastrophising; ruminating; spending hours examining her body for imperfections; tweaking social-media photos; drinking excessively; considered plastic surgery; isolating herself; overdose

'So, what was it about your relationship break-up that was making you feel depressed?' asks Dr Jim.

'That he was right to leave me,' replies Jill. 'He could see my physical imperfections and made the right choice.'

'But why would this make you feel depressed?' Dr Jim persists.

'Because I have these imperfections, I believe that I am ugly, ab-normal and a failure for not sorting them out,' she says sadly. 'I'm not worth staying with.' She then breaks down crying and admits that 'she was worthless and of no value to herself or any man'.

'And what was it about the break-up that made you feel anxious?' Dr Jim asks.

Jill replies that maybe she would never be able to eliminate her imperfections and end up alone. She also notes on questioning that she had struggled with fatigue, sleep and concentration on becoming anxious and depressed.

'So now let's examine what irrational belief was triggered by your relationship break-up that made you feel depressed,' says Dr Jim.

Following discussion, they agree that her belief was that 'because she was unable to eliminate her imperfections and hang on to her relationship, she was ugly, a failure and weird'. She also admits her belief that because of her body-image issues 'she was worthless', which was in her eyes just another sign that her self-esteem was low.

'And what irrational belief or demand were you making that made you feel anxious?' he asks.

Jill identifies that her main demand was that 'she must be able to eliminate her multiple imperfections; if not, she would be ugly, weird and a failure'.

They add this information to her ABC:

A – Activating Event:
- Trigger: recent break-up with boyfriend
- Inference/danger: her boyfriend was correct to leave her, because she was unable to eliminate her imperfections; she was ugly, a failure and weird. That she might never be able to resolve her body-image imperfections and never find a long-term partner

B – Belief/Demands: 'Because I am unable to eliminate my imperfections or retain my boyfriend, I am ugly, a failure and

weird.' 'I am worthless.' 'I must be able to eliminate my imperfections and find a long-term partner; if not, I am a failure.'

C – Consequences:
- Emotional reactions: depression and anxiety
- Physical reactions: stomach is in knots; muscle tension;
  sleep difficulties; fatigue
- Behaviour: catastrophising; ruminating; spending hours
  examining her body for imperfections; tweaking social-
  media photos; drinking excessively; considered plastic
  surgery; isolating herself; overdose

Dr Jim challenges Jill's thinking and behaviour.

They begin by Dr Jim strongly challenging her routine of constantly examining her body seeking imperfections. Was this really
helping her in her life or was it just increasing her anxiety and
depression?

Jill agrees but is unsure of how best to do this. Dr Jim promises
to give her exercises to assist her. They also agree that other behaviours, especially taking an overdose, have been unhelpful and
really upset her family. Jill also agrees to delist some of the social-
media sites which had led her down such dark roads.

'Let's now examine and challenge your "B", or your irrational
belief,' says Dr Jim. 'This took the form of a belief that "because
you could not eliminate all imperfections and hold on to your
boyfriend, you were a failure, ugly and weird". Is this belief rational or irrational?' he enquires.

Jill on consideration argues that it was probably irrational to
everyone else, but because of her body-image difficulties she still
believes that, for her, it was rational.

To counter such views, Dr Jim asks her to do the Rating Exercise. Jill rates herself on the lower end of the scale, decreasing

further when asked about her bodily imperfections. When Dr Jim challenges on what grounds or using what scale she was rating herself, Jill struggles.

'But am I not able to rate myself depending on how I look physically?' she queries.

This leads to a long discussion on whether a human being can be measured or not. Jill eventually agrees that there is no scale or book she could use to do so. Dr Jim then introduces her to the PC and how it tries to convince us when we are anxious or down that we are 'weak' or 'a failure' or 'worthless'. Jill admits that the PC was an 'old friend' who has been with her since her teens.

Dr Jim introduces her to Ellis's insights, and this leads to a long discussion where Jill is forced to accept that she has been self-rating herself mercilessly. Dr Jim then gives her the Unconditional Self-acceptance exercise to carry out for the following three months. He shows her how to challenge the PC on paper with the belief that she is 'ugly'; and 'a failure' and 'worthless' and she starts to understand why such self-definitions are both unhealthy and inaccurate.

She was especially taken with the thought that a human being could not be 'ugly' or 'beautiful' in themselves, but that physical appearances could technically be assessed as such. But as Dr Jim noted 'real beauty comes from within, not without'!

Jill now understands that self-esteem was not an issue, as human beings cannot be defined or measured in such a manner, so she agrees to cease trying to boost it to deal with her other issues. Dr Jim then challenges her irrational belief that 'she must eliminate all imperfections' and that 'she must find a long-term partner; if not, she is a failure'. He proceeds to ask her whether these demands are rational or irrational.

'But is my demand to be perfect and to eliminate all perfections not quite rational?' Jill asks.

'But is this an achievable demand?' asks Dr Jim.

After much discussion, Jill agrees that a healthier demand might be 'that she would prefer to have no imperfections, and indeed to find a long-term partner, but that these were out of her control'.

Dr Jim explains that when we are seeking control, one of the four things we are looking for is 100 per cent certainty. Another is 100 per cent perfection, along with order and security. 'So, what were you looking for here?' asks Dr Jim.

'I was seeking 100 per cent certainty and especially 100 per cent perfection,' Jill replies.

Following discussion, she accepts that it is completely unrealistic to demand 100 per cent certainty about this or indeed anything in life.

To challenge this demand, Dr Jim suggests the coin exercise detailed earlier.

'But what about 100 per cent perfection?' asks Dr Jim. 'Is this possible in real life'?

This leads to a frank conversation as to the irrationality of this demand.

'In real life,' he explains, 'absolute perfection is impossible for any of us to achieve. There will always be some imperfections, however small'. He also explains how those of us who seek total perfection are also falling into the trap of seeking out only imperfections in the world around us.

Jill begins to see where this is going. 'What you want me to understand is that I am only seeking imperfections in relation to my physical appearance whilst ignoring other positive aspects of my body?' she queries.

Dr Jim agrees.

'When suffering from body-image issues, many seek out small imperfections to do with some aspects of their face or body, but choose to ignore obvious positive, striking features, as these do not fit with their negative self-image. In real life there is no human being who has the perfect body,' he adds. 'It is a myth. We all have multiple small imperfections and it is this reality that you must learn to live with. We then consolidate this tendency to seek out small imperfections through our online behaviour,' he adds.

To assist her in emotionally integrating this information, Dr Jim gives Jill the perfectionism exercise already detailed, in which she would create and live with small daily imperfections and learn to adapt to them.

What followed was the most challenging four weeks of Jill's life. She found herself constantly keeping her head down, for example, as she laid off some make-up or left her hair in a mess. But gradually she learned to accept that she could live with small imperfections and, as a result, her anxiety levels began to fall. She also was surprised how few of her friends or colleagues even noticed the changes. As Dr Jim had good-humouredly assured her, 'None of us are as important as we think we are!'

Over the following months, she worked hard on developing unconditional self-acceptance and learning how to adapt and handle imperfections both bodily and indeed in other areas of her life. She began to relax more about her body image and ceased demanding that she must eliminate imperfections. She now accepted that all of us are imperfect but that that, too, is OK. Six months later, Jill is in a new relationship and because of all the hard work she had done on unconditional self-acceptance, her mental health is now blossoming.

Frank's story

Frank is twenty-eight and exists in a world of depression and shame, connected with his body-image issues, specifically his rotund shape, bordering on obesity. He had always struggled with body image and weight, the origins of both going back to his childhood. School had been a nightmare, with constant taunts and jibes about his appearance, driving him on a few occasions to self-harm in his late teens.

He now found himself locked into a vicious circle of self-loathing, addictive comfort eating and further weight gain, followed by more self-loathing. He had made numerous efforts to go on 'diets' throughout the previous decade, but quickly relapsed back into old habits. Frank lived on his own in an apartment and worked in a low-paid maintenance job at the local hospital.

Matters came to a head when he developed physical symptoms secondary to his obesity. He attended his family doctor with symptoms of shortness of breath, sleep difficulties and fatigue. He has a family history of heart disease, obesity and diabetes. Following investigations, his GP explains that Frank is a borderline diabetic who is at risk of obstructive sleep apnoea. He explains how his obesity was putting his physical health at risk, especially in view of his family history.

They also discuss his mental health, with Frank revealing how he has struggled with bouts of depression, also revealing that his self-esteem was very low, which in his eyes was the real problem. He also shared how ashamed he was both of his body image and his comfort eating. How he had worked with dieticians in the past to no avail. He also struggled to have a meaningful relationship as shame and disgust with himself prevented him from going there. This ended up with Frank feeling increasingly lonely and sadly commentating, 'If I were to go in the morning, I am not sure if anyone would notice.' He just felt 'stuck in a rut'!

His GP, concerned about his mental health, refers him to see Dr Jim as he senses that Frank will struggle to deal with his physical health issues unless his mental-health and self-esteem difficulties are managed.

Dr Jim listens to Frank's story and the latter finds him extremely empathetic. He offers to assist Frank in dealing with his difficulties, using CBT techniques. He tells him about rational and irrational beliefs and lays out the ABC concepts, explaining how they will employ this system to locate and manage his irrational beliefs. They agree to use his 'body image' as the trigger.

'How does this make you feel emotionally?' asks Dr Jim.

'I feel so ashamed,' he replies, 'and at times depressed, anxious and frustrated.'

'And what do you do when you feel ashamed or depressed about your body image?' asks Dr Jim.

'I just hide away from everyone, including friends and family,' Frank replies sadly. 'I have closed down all my social-media accounts, as I'm ashamed of what people would think of me.' He also admits to isolating himself at home in his apartment, stocking up with junk food and gallons of high-sugar drinks, aimlessly consuming vast amounts of food, refusing to look at himself in the mirror, avoiding meeting up with girls and on occasions even close friends, and ceasing any form of exercise. He also admits to physical symptoms of fatigue and struggling with sleep and concentration.

They add this information to Frank's ABC:

A – Activating Event:
- Trigger: negative body image
- Inference/danger:

B – Belief/Demands:

C – Consequences:
- Emotional reactions: shame; depression; anxiety and frustration

- Physical reactions: fatigue; poor concentration; sleep difficulties
- Behaviour: isolating himself from friends, family and potential relationships; shuts down his social-media sites; fills the apartment with junk food; aimlessly consuming large quantities of food; avoids looking at himself in the mirror

'What is it about your body image that is making you feel ashamed?' asks Dr Jim.

'I have always hated how I look physically,' explains Frank, 'and I cannot bear the thought that others will see how I look.'

'And what is it about how you look that you believe they will see?' Dr Jim asks.

For starters, I am grossly obese,' he answers, 'but that is only emphasising how rotund I am.' He explains that, when at school, he had been taunted with terms like 'fatso' and 'gross' and had never forgotten the deep wounds these words had opened.

'But why would you feel ashamed if people saw that you were overweight or had a rotund shape?'

Frank explains that he assumed that people, on seeing how obese he was, would end up judging him as 'weird' or 'gross' or 'weak and a failure' as he was unable to curtail his appetite.

'And what is it about your body image that is making you feel depressed?' asks Dr Jim.

'Because it reflects what I believe about myself,' he answers, 'that I am ugly, weak and weird. On occasions I even believe that I am worthless,' he adds with tears in his eyes. 'That is why I believe my self-esteem is low.'

'And what about it is making you feel anxious?' Dr Jim enquires.

'Because maybe I will always be like this, obese, gross and lonely,' answers Frank. He also admits that he is anxious that he might never eliminate his bodily imperfection.

'And frustrated?' Dr Jim asks.

Frank explains that his main frustration was with himself. 'I know that the only person who can change this is myself,' he adds, 'but I can't face the hard work and discomfort that dealing with my obesity will bring, though I still want to improve how I look physically.'

'Now let's examine what irrational beliefs were triggered by your poor body image,' says 'Dr Jim. 'These usually take the form of some irrational belief or absolute demand you are making about the trigger, which in this case related to your body image.'

After some discussion, Frank decides that in relation to his shame his main demand was that 'people would judge him as a freak or odd or weird, and he must accept their judgement'. In relation to his emotion of depression, his irrational belief was that 'because he was obese and rotund, he was weird, a failure and weak', even, on occasions, 'worthless'. He was also demanding in relation to his anxiety that 'he must not finish up morbidly obese and lonely; if this happens, he is a failure for allowing it to happen'. And that 'he must not exhibit any bodily imperfections. Behind his frustration, lay the demand that he 'must not suffer any discomfort in tackling his obesity'.

They add this information to Frank's ABC:

A – Activating Event:
- Trigger: negative body image
- Inference/danger: people will see him as obese and rotund and judge him as ugly, gross, weird and weak; because of his obesity and body image problems, he

is weird, a failure, weak and worthless; maybe it will always be like this and he will finish up alone and lonely; he wants to change the situation but is not prepared to accept the discomfort that this might entail

B – Belief/Demands: 'People will see that I am obese and judge me as weak, ugly and a failure.' 'Because of my body image issues and obesity, I am weird, ugly, weak and worthless.' 'I must not have any bodily imperfections – if I do, I am a failure.' 'I must not end up morbidly obese and lonely.' 'I should not have to put with the discomfort of tackling my obesity.'

C – Consequences:

- Emotional reactions: shame; depression; anxiety and frustration
- Physical reactions: fatigue; poor concentration; sleep difficulties
- Behaviour: isolating himself from friends, family and potential relationships; shuts down his social-media sites; fills the apartment with junk food; aimlessly consuming large quantities of food; avoids looking at himself in the mirror

Dr Jim then challenges Frank's thinking and behaviour.

They agree that his unhealthy behaviours are not assisting him in coping with the situation and are contributing to his shame and depression. How could isolating himself from friends and family or consuming large amounts of junk food, for example, assist him in his quest? Or avoiding mirrors? Dr Jim promises to return to his behaviour in relation to food later.

'Let's now examine and challenge your "B", or your irrational beliefs,' says Dr Jim. 'This initially took the form of an absolute demand that you must accept the negative judgements of "others". Is this demand rational or irrational?'

Frank believes it is completely rational.

'Am I not correct in assuming that others will quite rightly in my mind, judge me as ugly and weak?' he argues. 'And it is my belief that their negative assessments are more than justified.'

'But do we have to accept their negative judgements?' asks Dr Jim.

This leads to a long discussion on whether we must accept other people's assessments of us as human beings.

'We will return to this later,' Dr Jim assures him, 'but let's proceed to challenge another irrational belief: "that because you have body image issues and obesity, you are weird, ugly, weak and worthless". Is this belief rational or irrational?'

Once again, he meets opposition as Frank fully believes this belief was 'quite rational'!

To counter such entrenched views, Dr Jim asks Frank to do the Rating Exercise, where he rates himself on the lower end of the scale, decreasing further when questioned about his obesity and how he was managing it.

Dr Jim challenges on what grounds or using what scale, was Frank rating himself. This leads to a discussion on whether human beings can be measured or rated in such a manner. This is a light-bulb moment in Frank's life.

Dr Jim then introduces him to the PC and how it tries to convince us when we are anxious or down that we are 'weak' or 'a failure' or 'worthless'. And how, when ashamed, he is trying to convince us that others believe the same.

Frank can easily really relate to this voice. As they both agree, when he was feeling ashamed, it felt as if he was loaning out his PC to others, to beat him up with.

Dr Jim explores with Frank, Ellis's insights and Frank seeks advice on how best to apply these principles in his life.

Dr Jim gives him the Unconditional Self-acceptance exercise to carry out for the following three months. He also challenges the PC on paper, with the belief that he is 'weak' or 'ugly' or 'a failure' and most of all 'worthless'. Frank begins to understand that he could measure or rate his behaviour or skills, for example, but not himself as a person. He suddenly feels a great weight lifted off his shoulders. In relation to the belief that he is 'ugly', he is very taken by Dr Jim explaining how we often search the environment seeking proof that our irrational beliefs are true.

'So, what you are trying to get me to see is that I am only looking at imperfections in my bodily shape but ignoring positive aspects?' he asks, and Dr Jim agrees. This resonates strongly with Frank.

They agree that performing the Unconditional Self-acceptance Exercise for several months would greatly assist him in dealing with both his depression and shame. Frank agrees to perform this exercise diligently. He now understands that his obsession with self-esteem was also unhelpful and decides to drop the term from his vocabulary. As he notes wryly to Dr Jim, 'such concepts are best left to the graveyard of bad ideas'!

'Moving on to your demands that "you must not have any imperfections" and that "you must not end up morbidly obese and lonely", says Dr Jim. 'Are these rational or irrational?'

Following another discussion, Frank agrees that these are absolute demands and so not particularly rational. The rational belief or demand was that 'he would prefer not to end up morbidly obese or without a partner, but it was out of his control'.

Dr Jim explains that when we are seeking control in such situations, we are usually looking for 100 per cent certainty and perfection. They agree that neither is possible in real life. Frank is given the coin and perfection exercises detailed earlier, to emotionally integrate this insight.

By his next visit, Frank has worked hard at developing unconditional self-acceptance and busily challenging his longstanding tendency to seek out bodily imperfections. He is now ready at last to challenge his behaviour with respect to food.

They both agree that Frank has an addictive personality on top of his other body image issues. He agrees to attend a self-help food-addiction group and to see a dietician. As he is coming to terms with accepting himself as a person who happens to find himself addicted to junk food, Frank finds the group warm and empathetic and is open to their messages. He begins to embrace their twelve-step programme. All junk food is cleared out of his house and he begins with the assistance of the dietician to cook his own healthy meals and exercise regularly.

Within a year, Frank has lost over five stone and is in a new place emotionally. He no longer hides away, has reconnected with friends and family and is now dating Liz, who had also struggled with and overcome similar body-image issues. He is now increasingly 'comfortable in his own skin' – both emotionally and physically! Body image, like self-esteem, has finally been laid to rest.

11. UNCONDITIONAL SELF-ACCEPTANCE AND MENTAL HEALTH

Why Mental Health?

It is fitting to end our journey into the application of unconditional self-acceptance by examining its place in the management of common mental-health conditions. In earlier chapters we reviewed the vexed question of how self-esteem was assumed by many to be the root cause of mental-health difficulties such as depression, anxiety and addiction. How it was believed that those with low self-esteem were more likely to develop these conditions, especially depression, and how high self-esteem was apparently protective. This view is still embedded in the minds of large numbers of people. As discussed, the evidence for many of these beliefs is almost non-existent, with the root causes of such conditions originating from a variety of complex genetic, epigenetic and environmental factors.

When we move to the world of self-rating, an equally flawed but more accurate assessment of what many of us do in real life, there is a closer link with mental-health conditions such as anxiety, depression, body-image conditions and eating disorders. There can be little doubt that in depression, for example, due to reasons explored in a previous chapter, the PC can overpower our emotional mind with relentless self-critical messages. These can take on the form of persistent ruminations. These are, however, a 'symptom' of the condition and not the cause.

Some people assume that if they are experiencing these self-critical messages their 'self-esteem' must be low and that this explains their bout of depression. We now know that this is not the case. It is easy to see, however, in an era when self-esteem is as-cribed as the cause of almost anything negative relating to mental health, that this belief could have emerged.

The challenge

Negative self- and other-rating are related to a number of chal-lenging mental-health issues, some serious and others less so.

These include:

1. Depression at all stages of life, which usually comes in bouts lasting six to nine months at a time. This can in-clude post-natal depression, depression in the adolescent population from age fifteen to twenty-five, depression in the middle years and late-onset depression over the age of sixty.

2. In bipolar disorder, where our mood can swing from low to high, secondary to complex genetic and neurobiologi-cal causes, many of which are still poorly understood, self-rating can be intense during the depression phases of this condition. We now understand that this illness is almost completely biological in nature.

3. Anxiety, which can include general anxiety and social anxiety. At the heart of the former is a demand for abso-lute control of what happens to us in life and an irrational

belief that we are a failure if we cannot achieve this. At the heart of the latter is a belief that we must accept the negative self-ratings of others.

4. Eating disorders which are often associated with anxiety also contain at their heart elements of significant self-rating.

5. Self-harm can be the behavioural responses to periods of self- and other-rating, especially in younger age groups.

6. Toxic stress can also be linked to self-rating if our emotional responses to stressors is linked to either anxiety or depression.

7. Addiction can involve for some (but not all) intense self-rating in those fighting gambling, alcohol abuse and food addictions, for example, during periods when the addict is not involved in binges. This can set up a negative spiral of craving – feeding the addiction – self-rating and self-loathing, leading to low mood and a desire to feed the addiction further, and so on.

In all these cases, there can be periods of intense self- and other-rating, where the PC swamps the rational brain, leading to emotions of depression, anxiety, shame and guilt, often followed by unhealthy negative behaviours.

Unconditional Self-acceptance and Mental Health

The solution is to assist those struggling with many of these conditions to develop unconditional self-acceptance. To learn how to challenge the PC and put it back in its box. Clearly conditions such as depression, bipolar disorder, addiction and eating disorders may require different forms of therapies to assist them in recovery.

If this is not allied to unconditional self-acceptance, however, there is a significant risk of relapse. The PC is a bad enemy and one requiring direct confrontation to enable full recovery.

I believe that Ellis has left us, in the guise of unconditional self-acceptance, a powerful tool in our battle to prevent many of the mental-health issues noted above. If our primary, secondary and tertiary-level students could be taught this concept at the earliest possible opportunity, how much sadness, heartbreak, personal and family upsets could perhaps be avoided?

I believe it is not 'self-esteem' that underlies these conditions but rather 'self- and other-rating'. If we could develop and practise unconditional self-acceptance, many of us could become emotionally more resilient and better able to nurture and safeguard our mental health. If we could put as much effort into teaching our young people this concept as we are now doing in trying to 'boost' their mythical self-esteem, the mental-health landscape of the future could be transformed.

We would also achieve the additional bonus of teaching them how to take responsibility for their behaviour and skills. And we could challenge them to get up and try again when they – as we all do – fail in relation to both. If all of us work together on this project, maybe we can finally bring Ellis's dream to fruition.

Carl's story

Carl is thirty-four and has struggled with anxiety since his early teens. He comes from a family background where both parents were equally anxious. He spends his time worrying and catastrophising, constantly fatigued as a result. Like his mum, Carl is a perfectionist and, like his father, a chronic procrastinator. This was beginning to cause difficulties at work as he was always late with assignments. He was reasonably comfortable in social situations but dreaded giving presentations.

Then Carl's world began to implode. His partner of five years, Maeve, informed him that she was considering leaving if he didn't do something to change his persistent catastrophising. His boss then sent an email noting that, on return from a trip abroad, he planned to have a 'serious' meeting with Carl. Carl's anxiety levels soared and, out of nowhere, panic attacks arrived. He was ashamed when, following a panic attack at work, he found himself in A&E, where a tired consultant assured him that he is physically well but needed to do something about his anxiety levels.

Carl attends his family doctor, seeking a 'magic tablet' to assist him in dealing with his anxiety and panic attacks. He also conveys Maeve's message, that Carl had better do something about his self-esteem, which she believes underlies his current difficulties. His GP reassures him that he does not require medication but would benefit from attending a colleague, Dr Jim, who could help him acquire skills to manage his anxiety.

Carl attends Dr Jim and pours out his story. They agree that he has a mixture of three types of anxiety, ranging from acute anxiety in the form of panic attacks, to general anxiety and social anxiety in the form of performance anxiety regarding his presentations.

'But what about my self-esteem issues?' asks Carl. 'Does my poor self-esteem not lie at the heart of all these difficulties?' Dr Jim promises to return to this issue later. He offers to assist Carl to deal with all his issues, using CBT techniques. He tells him about rational and irrational beliefs and lays out the ABC concepts, explaining how they will employ this system to locate and manage his irrational beliefs.

They begin with Dr Jim assisting Carl to banish his panic attacks by using the Flooding technique mentioned earlier. Carl is relieved to discover that the acute physical symptoms he had been experiencing were not dangerous but just uncomfortable. He was not going to die, lose control or go mad, and his symptoms were due simply to an adrenaline rush. He begins to apply the Flooding technique and his panic attacks begin to wane and eventually disappear. Never again will he worry about having panic attacks, as he now knows what to do.

Now Carl is ready to tackle his general anxiety. They agree to use the recent twin stressors – 'the email from his boss and the threat from Maeve to leave' – as the trigger.

'How did both events make you feel emotionally?' asks Dr Jim.

'Incredibly anxious,' Carl replies, 'almost panicky.'

'And how did this make you feel physically?'

'I felt so tired,' Carl replies. 'At night I would find myself increasingly tense, yet unable to fall asleep. When I did sleep, my jaws would ache in the morning from clenching my teeth,' he adds, 'and I really struggled to concentrate.'

'And what did you do when you became anxious?' queries Dr Jim.

Carl admits to spending countless hours worrying and catastrophising, firstly about Maeve leaving and then later about what the boss had in store for him. He began to comfort eat; spent hours looking up job opportunities in case he was let go; tried excessively to please Maeve, secretly checking her social-media sites and phone to reassure himself that she was not seeing someone else; rang his mum to seek reassurance; and procrastinated further in relation to assignments due.

They add this information to Carl's ABC:

A – Activating Event:
- Trigger: partner Maeve threatening to leave; email from boss to arrange 'serious' meeting
- Inference/danger:

B – Belief/Demands:

C – Consequences:
- Emotional reactions: anxiety and panic
- Physical reactions: fatigue; sleep difficulties; teeth grinding; poor concentration
- Behaviour: spending hours worrying and catastrophising about both issues; checking out job possibilities if fired; trying to excessively please partner Maeve; checking her social media and phone; ringing his mum for reassurance; comfort eating; procrastinating further with work assignments

Dr Jim then asks Carl, 'What was it about Maeve threatening to end the relationship and the email from your boss that made you feel anxious? What danger were you assigning to both?'

'In relation to Maeve, I worried that maybe she is going to leave me,' he answers.

'And why would this make you feel anxious?' persists Dr Jim.

'It would be a disaster,' says Carl. 'I have invested so much in this relationship. If this relationship were to finish, I will never meet someone like her again.'

'And suppose you didn't?' asks Dr Jim.

'I can see myself already,' replies Carl, 'a lonely, embittered, middle-aged man, much to be pitied by those around me.'

'What about the email from your boss?' asks Dr Jim.

'I just know it is bad news,' replies Carl. 'Even the tone of the email seemed ominous.'

'But what do you think is going to happen at this proposed meeting?'

'I know he is unhappy with my constant delays in completing major assignments,' explains Carl, 'so I assume that it is time for him to let me go.'

'And why would that make you anxious?' asks Dr Jim.

'Maybe I would never find another post like this,' he answers, 'especially if I had a negative reference due to my acknowledged difficulties in completing assignments. My whole world is going up in flames,' he adds. 'If I lose this job, maybe that will trigger Maeve to leave. Who would want to be around me if I did lose my job? A loser and a failure.'

'Is this what you would think about yourself if you did lose your job or indeed Maeve?'

Carl agrees sadly: 'If either of these do occur, I would believe that I was both of those but especially a failure.'

'So now let's examine what irrational belief was triggered by the email from your boss and the threat from Maeve to leave,' says Dr Jim. 'This usually takes the form of some irrational belief or absolute demand you are making about the trigger, which in this case related to both events,' he explains.

After some discussion, Carl decides that his demands were that 'he must not lose his job' and that 'Maeve must not leave him' and that 'if either of these do occur, he would be a failure'. Dr Jim explains that it was these demands that triggered his emotion of anxiety.

They add this information to finish Carl's ABC:

A – Activating Event:
- Trigger: partner Maeve threatening to leave; email from boss to arrange 'serious' meeting

- Inference/danger: maybe Maeve is going to leave, if this happens it will be a catastrophe, he will never be able to meet someone like her again, he will end up lonely and bitter; his boss is going to fire him at the upcoming meeting as a result of his procrastinating; if Maeve does leave or he loses his job, he would be a failure

B – Belief/Demands: 'I must not lose my job: if I do, I am a failure.' 'Maeve must not leave me: if this happens, I am a failure for letting it happen.'

C – Consequences:

- Emotional reactions: anxiety and panic
- Physical reactions: fatigue; sleep difficulties; teeth grinding; poor concentration
- Behaviour: spending hours worrying and catastrophising about both issues; checking out job possibilities if fired; trying to excessively please partner Maeve; checking her social media and phone; ringing his mum for reassurance; comfort eating; procrastinating further with work assignments

Dr Jim then challenges Carl's thinking and behaviour.

They begin with his behaviour. How could spending hours catastrophising or checking out jobs online while still employed assist him in dealing with the situation? Could trying to excessively please Maeve or checking her social media advance the situation? They agree that his procrastination would have to be challenged, with Dr Jim agreeing to assist him with this task later. They also discuss lifestyle issues such as exercise and proper nutrition, with Carl agreeing to challenge many of these unhealthy behaviours.

'Let's now examine and challenge your "B", or your irrational belief,' says Dr Jim. 'This took the form of some absolute demands "that Maeve must not leave you and that you must not lose your job" and that "if either of these occurred, that you are a failure". Are these demands rational or irrational?'

After some discussion, they agree that a more rational or healthier demand might be that 'Carl would prefer not to lose his job, and that Maeve would not leave him, but that both are out his control'. This leads to a discussion on the importance of control in his life.

Dr Jim explains that when seeking control, we are usually seeking 100 per cent certainty. They agree that this is an impossible demand to achieve in real life. Dr Jim suggests the coin exercise detailed earlier, to learn how to challenge this demand and Carl agrees to put it into practice.

They also discuss how Carl is catastrophising in relation to both Maeve's threat and the upcoming meeting with his boss. Had he any real evidence that Maeve was going to leave him, or that he would never meet anyone else if this happened, or that he would end up lonely and bitter?

Carl admits that this was what occurred every time he became anxious about anything that 'I just can't get out of my head'. To assist him with this, Dr Jim gives him an exercise called the Spilt Milk Exercise (detailed in *Emotional Resilience*) which encourages him to write down the trigger and his conclusions when he finds himself catastrophising, for the following two months, and then seek out evidence on paper whether they were true or not. Carl finds himself energised at the prospect of 'putting the monster in his head to bed' and agrees to perform this exercise.

Dr Jim then challenges the belief that if Maeve left or he lost his job 'he was a failure'. He does the Rating Exercise with Carl who finds himself rating himself up or down depending on what question he was asked.

'But can we rate or measure a human being at all, is there a scale or table to do so?' asks Dr Jim. This was a watershed moment for Carl: that there was in practice no scale or measurement to do so. Dr Jim then introduces him to the PC and how it tries to convince us when we are anxious or down that we are 'a failure' or 'weak' or 'worthless'. Carl could really relate to this inner critical voice. 'He has always been there,' he admits, 'as long as I can remember.'

Dr Jim introduces Carl to Ellis's insights, and he is blown away by their beauty and simplicity. 'But how can I learn to apply them in my life?' he asks. To assist him, Dr Jim gives Carl the Unconditional Self-acceptance exercise to carry out for the following three months. He then shows him how to challenge the PC on paper with the belief that he is 'a failure' and 'worthless'.

Carl grasps that whether he is successful or not at holding down his job or retaining his relationship does not define who he is as a human being. He is also energised by the concept that 'If he did fail at these tasks or indeed any task, the only failure was not getting back up and trying again.'

They have a revealing discussion on whether a human being can be rated as 'worthless' and how the term 'self-esteem' was in practice a mythical concept which was of little use in his life. Carl couldn't wait to get back to discuss this insight with Maeve. He would never again think of the word 'worthless' in the same way and vowed to challenge his PC at every opportunity.

Over the next six months, Carl works hard on performing the various exercises that Dr Jim had suggested. He is managing uncertainty better and slowly reducing his catastrophising. He is now increasingly comfortable in his own skin. His anxiety levels have plummeted, his energy levels have risen, and his sleep and cognition improve. Maeve is delighted with the changes he has made to his life and is now applying some of the techniques Carl shared with her in her own life. They are making plans to make their relationship 'official' and considering starting a family.

Carl later reveals to Dr Jim how pleasantly surprised he was when his boss on his return offered him a promotion with extra responsibilities but on a higher salary. Dr Jim finally assists him to challenge his procrastination and to become comfortable giving presentations (the techniques of which are laid out in *Emotional Resilience*). Acquiring these skills completes Carl's transformation.

Sally's story

Sally is thirty-nine and has been in a long-term relationship with Dave for the previous decade. They were both busy and successful with careers in the city and had decided three years previously to have a child. This was not as simple a task as both assumed. Finally, after three anxious and stressful years, including two trials of IVF, Sally becomes pregnant and, following a difficult birth, delivered a baby daughter, Megan.

Both were overjoyed with the new arrival. Unfortunately, both sets of parents and most of their siblings are scattered geographically. They found themselves isolated with little Megan. Sally had arranged to take the first six months off to care for Megan, but Dave must go back to work after the first week at home. Sally's mum was with her for the first month, but then had to return home as her dad is unwell. Sally found herself stranded, without support, with Megan.

After the initial euphoria of the new arrival had worn off, Sally's mood dropped. She was completely exhausted following a difficult birth and struggled from the beginning with breastfeeding Megan. She had heard so much about the importance of breastfeeding from midwives and friends. They were so enthusiastic and positive about its beneficial effects for mum and baby. She did have some initial visits from the public health nurse but, despite this, Megan was not thriving. Sally found herself increasingly exhausted from lack of sleep, with her baby's on-demand feeding. Her mood dropped further. Dave did what he could, but Sally felt helpless and guilty that her baby was not thriving.

Matters came to a head during the six-week check-up when it was discovered that Megan was not gaining weight. A decision was made to switch to bottle feeding. Sally was devastated. She had failed her baby in this, the simplest of tasks, and one that many of her peers had been so successful at. Her mood dropped further but Sally hid it from Dave and from any friends that called to see her. She presented a public face that all was well. Even when her mum rang, she pretended that everything was fine.

Then, in week seven, the screaming began. For seemingly no obvious reason, her baby began to cry inconsolably and writhe in pain. It began after 6 p.m. but after a week or so seemed to occur earlier and earlier in the day. After several visits to her GP, who reassured her that it was infant colic and would in time subside, Sally understood there was nothing physically wrong with Megan. But the crying seemed relentless, putting a further strain on her mood.

Matters worsened as she noted on social media how other mothers were putting up pictures of themselves and their babies, with both seeming happy and content. Some innocent comments about the joys of breastfeeding made her increasingly guilty and depressed. What was wrong with her? Then one of her friends, Jane, came to visit her, enthusing as to how wonderful she had found motherhood and how positive an experience it had been for her and her baby. Sally put on a brave face but inside was crumbling. She was such a failure.

From then on, her mood began to significantly drop. Dave became concerned that she was withdrawing emotionally from both Megan and himself. Sally kept denying there was a problem as she was ashamed to be feeling the way she was. With a loving partner and a beautiful daughter, how could she admit that she was depressed and struggling? And still Megan's crying continued, and Sally's sleep and appetite deteriorated further. She knew she was no longer bonding properly with Megan, making her increasingly guilty and depressed. She found herself withdrawing completely and struggling with concentration and memory.

Sally began to wonder if there really was a place for Megan and herself in the world and became increasingly distressed at having such thoughts. Thankfully help in the form of her mother arrived, alerted with a mother's intuition that matters were not right.

Sally broke down and shared with her mum how bad she was feeling. It was a watershed moment. Her mum revealed to Dave and Sally how she too experienced a significant bout of post-natal depression following her first pregnancy.

With their assistance, Sally attends her family doctor and after discussion with her, they decide on a course of action. Her mum would stay with her for a period to give her some support, Dave would take over night feeds and Sally agrees to see a specialist who advises her to consider a course of drug therapy to lift her mood, which has by this stage fallen dramatically. They agree when her mood begins to lift that she might attend a colleague, Dr Jim, for some talk therapy.

Within three to four weeks, Sally notices that her mood is lifting and that she is bonding better with Megan (who is by now crying less and becoming more settled as the weeks pass). Sally is also sleeping better, and she and Megan are putting on weight. She also notes that she is able to focus and concentrate better and is not as fatigued.

Her specialist refers her to Dr Jim. Her mum suggests that she might ask him to demonstrate some techniques to boost her self-esteem, as she believes that this is the basis of Sally's difficulties. She adds that her own bouts of depression had not been solely confined to that one post-natal episode but had recurred subsequently on several occasions during her life.

Dr Jim listens to Sally's story quietly and she finds him extremely empathetic. He explains that her story is common, which Sally finds surprising as she believed that it was only 'her' that was the 'freak'. Although improving in mood, they agree that she is still struggling with negative thoughts about herself and what has happened.

Dr Jim then suggests that they might use some CBT techniques to deal with her issues. He tells Sally about rational and irrational beliefs and lays out the ABC concepts, explaining how they will employ this system to locate and manage her irrational beliefs. They decide to use Megan's difficulties with thriving as the trigger.

'How did this make you feel emotionally?' Dr Jim asks.

Sally begins to become quite emotional.

'I felt so guilty,' she admits with tears forming, 'and so depressed and ashamed.'

'And what was your behaviour when you felt guilty, depressed and ashamed?' he asks.

Sally explains that she began to cry more, withdraw from both Dave and Megan emotionally, ceased contacting friends, especially those with children, hid how she felt from her mum, considered self-harm and 'couldn't stop the thoughts going around and around in my head about how awful I was and the damage I was doing to my beautiful daughter'. They also note how she stopped eating and lost weight and struggled with fatigue, sleep and concentration.

They add this information to Sally's ABC:

A – Activating Event:
- Trigger: newborn baby Megan struggling to thrive
- Inference/danger:

B – Belief/Demands:

C – Consequences:
- Emotional reactions: depression; shame and guilt
- Physical reactions: fatigue; difficulties concentrating; losing weight
- Behaviour: ruminating continuously; stopped eating; isolating herself from family and friends; hiding how she feels from mum; withdrawing emotionally from baby and husband; checking social media of friends with small babies; struggled with sleep; considered self-harm

'So, what was it about Megan not thriving that caused you to feel guilty?' asks Dr Jim.

'I believed that I was letting her down,' replies Sally. 'The job of a good mother is to be able to give her baby the best nutrition, which all the experts have told me is in breast milk.'

'But why would you feel guilty if you were unable to meet such needs?' he asks.

Sally explains that other mothers seemed to have no difficulty in breastfeeding, so she believed that she was letting Megan down when she could not do likewise.

She also admits that she felt guilty about not having anticipated such difficulties and prepared for them when pregnant, for not being able to calm her baby down when crying and for 'letting her husband and child down by getting depressed'.

'So, what was it about Megan not thriving that caused you to feel depressed?' asks Dr Jim.

'I believed that I was a complete failure,' Sally replies, 'a useless mother, not worth anything to Megan or indeed anyone else.' She adds that her inability to cope with her persistent crying only confirmed that she was useless. 'Wouldn't any decent mother be able to comfort her baby when distressed like this? And as for getting a bout of post-natal depression,' she adds, 'that was the final straw. Instead of being able to enjoy this wonderful experience with Dave and Megan, I crumble and end up having to take tablets. I am so weak and worthless.' At this stage the tears are rolling down her cheeks. Dr Jim reassures her that it was common to think like this when our mood is down and that they would return to these issues later.

'So, what was it, Sally, about Megan not thriving that caused you to feel ashamed?' asks Dr Jim.

'I was so ashamed that Dave and my mum and all my friends and colleagues who called to see me would see that I was unable to cope with being a new mum,' she replies. 'I have always been the "strong one" that everyone else looks to for support. How could I let them know that I was unable to look after the needs of my own daughter, both in terms of breastfeeding and comforting her when crying?'

'But why would you feel ashamed if they did find out?' Dr Jim asks.

'Because they would judge me as the weak, incompetent, useless person I believe I am,' she says sadly.

'So now let's examine what irrational belief or demand was triggered by Megan struggling to thrive and your inability to calm her down when crying that made you feel guilty,' says Dr Jim.

After some discussion, they agree that her main demand was 'she should have been able to know before she got pregnant that these issues would arise and should have been able to prepare better for them'. They also agree that she was demanding that 'she should have been able to breastfeed her child and calm her down when crying'.

'And what irrational belief was triggered when these triggers made you feel depressed?' asks Dr Jim.

Sally finds this question easy to answer. She decided that because of these issues she was useless, a failure, weak, and believed she was abnormal as all other mothers could cope with ease.

'And what irrational belief or demand was triggered by Megan struggling to thrive that made you feel ashamed?' asks Dr Jim. They agree that her main demand here was that others would judge her as weak and a failure and that she would have to accept their judgement.

They add this information to complete Sally's ABC:

A – Activating Event:
- Trigger: newborn baby struggling to thrive
- Inference/danger: that she was letting Megan down by being unable to breastfeed or soothe her when crying; that she was not well enough prepared for her arrival or the above would not have occurred; by developing post-natal depression she was letting Megan and Dave her partner down; that she was a failure, weak, useless and abnormal for not being able to breastfeed or calm her baby down when crying and for developing post-natal depression and having to take medication; that others might find out that she had struggled feeding or calming down her child or that she had developed post-natal depression and judge her accordingly

B – Belief/Demands: 'I should have known when pregnant that these difficulties might arise and been able to avoid them.' 'I should be able to breastfeed and calm down Megan when distressed.' 'Because I am unable to breastfeed or calm my baby down and because I have developed post-natal depression, I am a failure, weak, useless, worthless and abnormal.' 'Others will discover how poor a mother I am and that I have post-natal depression and judge me as weak and a failure.'

C – Consequences:

- Emotional reactions: depression; shame and guilt
- Physical reactions: fatigue; difficulties concentrating; losing weight
- Behaviour: ruminating continuously; stopped eating; isolating herself from family and friends; hiding how she feels from mum; withdrawing emotionally from baby and husband; checking social media of friends with small babies; struggled with sleep; considered self-harm

Dr Jim then challenges her thinking and behaviour.

They begin with Dr Jim strongly challenging her behaviour. How was spending long periods ruminating, ceasing eating or hiding information from her husband, mother and colleagues, for example, going to help her manage her depression and shame? Or considering self-harm? They agree that these and other unhealthy behaviours are counterproductive, and Sally agrees to challenge them.

'Let's now examine and challenge your "B", or your irrational belief or demand that was making you feel guilty,' says Dr Jim. 'This took the form of a belief that "you should have been able to predict that you would struggle with breastfeeding or calming down Megan when distressed and that you might develop post-natal depression?' he inquires.

Sally struggles with this.

'Are you saying that I could not have prevented this happening?' she replies.

'Do you have the "sight" or the ability to see into the future?' he asks.

Sally smiles.

'That would be a useful skill to have,' she replies, 'but I missed out on that one.' This leads to a discussion on how, when we are guilty about anything, we are trying to rewrite what happened to achieve a different result. They agree that is impossible, for example, to know whether one will struggle or not with breastfeeding or how severely a child may suffer colic in advance. They also agree that it is impossible to predict whether one gets post-natal depression or not. But Dr Jim is especially challenging about her demand that she should be able to breastfeed like all other mothers. 'Is this demand rational?' he enquires.

After some discussion, Sally learns that many women struggle in this area, and despite every effort and good intention must switch to a formula milk. She begins to understand that she has been self-flagellating without reason.

'And what about your belief that because you struggled with breastfeeding and calming down a child with three-month colic, you are a failure and useless?' asks Dr Jim. 'Is this rational or irrational?'

Sally is adamant that she was indeed a failure and useless and worthless and weak because she had struggled with these issues. To counter such views, Dr Jim asks her to do the Rating Exercise. Sally finds herself harshly rating herself well down on the scale and thought others also rated her quite low, especially when asked about the effects of her struggles with the above.

This leads to a long discussion on whether a human being could be measured or not. Sally finally admits that there was no scale or book she could use to do so. Dr Jim then introduces her to the PC and how it tries to convince us when we are anxious or down that we are 'weak' or 'a failure' or 'worthless'. Sally, having lived with this voice for the previous few months, is easily able to relate to her inner critic.

Dr Jim introduces her to Ellis's insights, and she is quite moved by the core messages contained within them. Dr Jim then gives Sally the Unconditional Self-acceptance exercise to carry out for the following three months. He shows her how to challenge the PC on paper with the belief that she is 'a failure' and 'weak' and 'worthless' and 'useless' and 'worthless' and she begins to understand why such self-definitions are both unhealthy and inaccurate.

They spend some time discussing why she felt she was 'abnormal'.

'Do all mums struggle for the first six to twelve months following the arrival of a new child into the house?' he asks.

Sally argues that they don't, but Dr Jim strongly disputes this with her.

'Most mothers and indeed couples are blown to pieces for the first year,' he explains. 'The mum is exhausted after the pregnancy and especially the delivery and then arrives home to an empty house apart from their partner and, if they're lucky, a grandparent for a short period. They don't get enough sleep for at least six months. They are isolated and suddenly detached from normal routines, families and work colleagues, often becoming extremely lonely. Their whole world has suddenly been turned upside-down. This is worsened if the mum is not close, as is so often the case in modern life, to support structures such as parents, siblings or close friends.' He adds wryly that 'Armageddon is a useful description of what happens in most households during the first year of their child's life'.

Sally suddenly begins to identify what Dr Jim is trying to assist her in seeing.

'You are saying that I have been believing irrationally that it is "me" who is abnormal whereas in practice it is the situation?' she asks, and he agrees.

'It is this belief that – together with the extreme stress and lack of sleep, and an absence of key support structures – can trigger a bout of post-natal depression.'

This is a watershed moment for Sally. In a flash, she finds a weight lifted off her shoulders. It was normal for her to struggle in this way and a relief to know she was not abnormal nor weak nor a failure. She agrees to challenge her PC on paper for the months that would follow.

They also discuss and dismiss her ideas in relation to being 'worthless' or 'lacking in self-esteem'. A human being's worth could not be measured in such ways. She was instead a special, unique person who now had a beautiful daughter along with a loving partner. She just had to learn how to accept herself as such.

When they begin to discuss her demands on shame and how she must accept other people's ratings of her, Sally quickly jumps in to say that she now accepted that this was completely irrational and understood why 'I am back playing the rating game', and Dr Jim agrees.

Over the next few months, Sally, whose mood gradually returned to normal, begins to put what she has learned into practice. She now understands that the chaos that heralds the arrival of a new baby into a relationship is normal. When she decides to join a mother and baby group in the area on the advice of one of her friends, all is suddenly revealed as one by one they all begin to admit how difficult many of them are finding this period. They all begin to support one another.

Sally, following several months practising unconditional self-acceptance, has now become increasingly comfortable in her own skin, and is busy sharing some of her insights with the mother and baby group, with most of them deciding they too would like to learn more.

She is now bonding with Megan, who has ceased to suffer from bouts of colic. Instead she is now teething badly and back crying again at night. Sally now realises that this is the life of the new parent, that she is not alone in her struggles, and finds herself coping better.

Nine months later, she is off all medication and completely well, her bout of post-natal depression a distant memory.

Martin's story

Martin comes to see Dr Jim on the advice of his college counsellor, with a history of low-grade depression and significant frustration. He is a twenty-four-year-old postgraduate who sees himself on the fast track to academic stardom. Blocking him is his one weakness, as he explains to Dr Jim, namely his inability to come to terms with his crippling social anxiety. Martin has always believed he was the best, the message having been drilled into him from an early age by well-meaning but misguided parents.

They had praised his every achievement, however small, and chose to overlook any mishaps. In their mind, boosting their child's self-esteem was the short cut to a successful career like his father's, a senior barrister. Whilst in secondary school, however, Martin was publicly shamed by a teacher in front of his peers and this set in train future difficulties with social anxiety.

He admits to Dr Jim that he was frustrated with himself in being unable to sort out his difficulties in this area. He also reveals that it was inhibiting his ability to attract and maintain relationships with the opposite sex and that this too was frustrating him intensely. He hopes that Dr Jim might assist him to boost his self-esteem further, as his father has explained that this might be the problem.

Dr Jim listens quietly and then offers to assist Martin to deal with all his issues, using some CBT techniques. He tells him about rational and irrational beliefs and lays out the ABC concepts, explaining how they will employ this system to locate and manage his irrational beliefs. They decide to use a typical example in which 'Martin was invited to a party, where he would be meeting a mixture of people he knew and some he didn't' as the trigger. To make matter worse, there would be some girls he had not met.

'And how did this make you feel emotionally?' asks Dr Jim.

'Extremely anxious,' replies Martin, 'but also embarrassed, and later I became depressed and frustrated.'

'And how did you feel physically when you were anxious about this upcoming social event?' Dr Jim asks.

Martin admits that the closer it got to the time of the party, the more 'his heart began to beat faster, stomach in knots, shaky, sweating, dry mouth, muscles coiled like a spring and a sense of impending doom'.

'On occasions I even began to blush,' he adds shamefacedly.

'And what did you do when you became anxious about going to the party?' Dr Jim enquires.

This leads to a discussion of the typical behaviours that Martin has learned to employ over the years. He would of course avoid the party if possible, but that was rarely an option.

He then admits to a complex ritual of rehearsing in front of a mirror before he left the house, heading straight for the bar when he got there, hanging around near the edges of groups, trying to avoid initiating conversations, rehearsing in his head what he might say if engaged in conversation, monitoring the faces of those around him at the party to see how he was coming across and then doing the dreaded post-mortem after the event. It really was exhausting and frustrated him completely.

They add this information to Martin's ABC:

A – Activating Event:
  • Trigger: meeting up with mixed group of friends at party
  • Inference/danger:
B – Belief/Demands:
C – Consequences:
  • Emotional reactions: anxiety; shame; depression and frustration
  • Physical reactions: heart beating faster; shaking; sweating; stomach in knots; breathing faster; dry mouth; muscles tense; and sense of impending doom
  • Behaviour: avoid if possible; rehearsal in front of mirror; heads straight to bar for alcohol; stays at the edge of groups; tries to avoid initiating conversation; rehearses what he is going to say before he says it; monitors faces for reactions and does a post-mortem on how badly he performed

'So, what is it about going to the party that was making you anxious?' asks Dr Jim. 'What danger were you assigning to it?'

Martin on reflection wonders if it was that 'people might see that I was anxious?'

'But what do you think they will see that might make them assume you are anxious?' asks Dr Jim.

Martin thinks the reply is obvious.

'I am assuming they would see the way I was presenting physically,' he replies. 'Shaking, blushing, sweating, fidgety and clearly ill at ease.'

'Is there anything else they might see that might make them assume you were anxious?' asks Dr Jim. On further reflection Martin adds that 'they might see that I am always hanging around the edge of the group and uncomfortable with conversation'.

Dr Jim summarises these dangers.

'So, you are saying that people might see some physical signs of anxiety and that, combined with this, you are uneasy or uncomfortable holding down a conversation?' he says, and Martin agrees.

Dr Jim notes with interest that Martin finds people in general 'boring', which adds to his conversational difficulties.

'But why would you be anxious that people would see that you are anxious at all?' asks Dr Jim.

'My main danger is that they will end up judging me, if they saw me in that state,' answers Martin.

'And why would you be ashamed or embarrassed if people did judge you because they saw that you were anxious?' asks Dr Jim.

'Because they would judge me as "weak", "a failure socially" and above all odd, different or "weird",' he replies.

'But why would the upcoming party make you frustrated?' asks Dr Jim. 'What inferences were you making?

'I was frustrated mainly with myself that I was unable to deal with my "weakness" myself,' Martin replies. 'I also get frustrated that I have to go through the hassle of these silly, boring social situations to meet people, especially potential dates,' he elaborates further. 'Surely there must be a short cut, a simpler route to achieving my goal?'

'And what is it about the upcoming party that would make you feel emotionally depressed?' asks Dr Jim.

'Because it only highlights my failure in this area,' Martin explains. 'Only weak people struggle in social situations, which even a child can manage.' He adds that he is struggling specifically to deal with his failure 'as he was successful in every other sphere of his life'.

'So now let's examine what irrational beliefs and absolute demands were triggered by this upcoming party,' says Dr Jim.

Following a lengthy discussion, they agree that the demand behind his anxiety was that 'he must not be exposed to any situation where people might see that he was anxious'. Behind his shame was the demand that 'others in the social situation will judge him as weak and he must accept their judgment'. Behind his emotion of depression that 'because he was unable to cope with social situations, he was weak and weird'. Finally, they agree that behind his emotion of frustration lie the twin demands that 'he should not have to suffer any discomfort or hassle' and that 'social situations, conversations and indeed the world must change to suit him'! Martin finds the latter extremely challenging but is forced to admit that 'it is an accurate reflection of how he looked at the world and life itself'.

They add this information to complete Martin's ABC:

A – Activating Event:
- Trigger: meeting up with mixed group of friends at party
- Inference/danger: that he will become anxious physically at the party; that people will notice that he is sweating, blushing, shaky, fidgety and staying at edge of groups;

that they will notice he is poor at conversation; that they will judge him as he is judging himself, as weak, a failure and weird; that it was distressing him that he was not able to cope with such situations; that there has to be a simpler, easier means to meet people than boring, silly social occasions such as the party

B – Belief/Demands: 'I must not be exposed to any situation where people can see I am anxious.' 'People will judge me as weak and weird and I must accept their judgment.' 'Because I am unable to be comfortable in social situations, I am weak, a failure and weird.' 'I should not have to suffer any discomfort.' 'Social situations, conversations and indeed the world itself, must change to suit me.'

C – Consequences:

- Emotional reactions: anxiety; shame; depression and frustration
- Physical reactions: heart beating faster; shaking; sweating; stomach in knots; breathing faster; dry mouth; muscles tense; and sense of impending doom
- Behaviour: avoid if possible; rehearsal in front of mirror; heads straight to bar for alcohol; stays at the edge of groups; tries to avoid initiating conversation; rehearses what he is going to say before he says it; monitors faces for reactions and does a post-mortem on how badly he performed

Dr Jim then challenges Martin's thinking and behaviour.

After some discussion, Martin realises that most of his behaviours are unhealthy and only contributing to his anxiety and shame. How could avoiding the party or taking part in the safety behaviours mentioned above assist him in any way to deal with his social anxiety? Dr Jim promises to teach him more effective techniques to manage his difficulties.

'Let's now examine and challenge your "B", or the irrational belief or total demand that underlined your anxiety,' says Dr Jim. 'This took the form of a demand that you "must never be exposed to any situation where people might see you were anxious". Is this demand rational or irrational?'

They agree that it was completely irrational as it is an impossible demand to achieve in real life.

They then turn their attention to the irrational belief/demands that underline his emotions of shame. This takes the guise of an absolute demand that 'people would not judge Martin as weak or a failure as if they do, he would be forced to accept their judgement'.

'Is this belief rational?' asks Dr Jim knowingly.

Martin reluctantly accepts this demand as being irrational, along with his belief that he was weak or a failure or weird.

To assist him in how best to dispute this demand, Dr Jim discusses the world of rating and asks Martin to perform the Rating Exercise. Martin finds himself playing the rating game both in relation to his own personal rating and how he believes others are rating him. His personal rating is up near ninety-seven but when asked if he had made a mess of a social situation it drops to eighty, which he finds intolerable.

'But can we rate or measure a human being at all? Is there a scale or table to do so?' asks Dr Jim.

This leads to an intense discussion, with Martin finding it especially challenging that he is forbidden to rate himself on the upper end of the scale as this is where he feels he belongs.

'Are you saying that I am not allowed to rate myself highly?' he asks. 'This is what I have been taught to do.'

'If this is working so well for you,' answers Dr Jim, 'then why are you here?'

Martin is forced to accept that rating has not brought much happiness into his life. Dr Jim introduces him to Ellis's insights, which he reluctantly agrees to explore further. They discuss the role of the PC, with Martin revealing that the latter only became active if he messed up socially. Dr Jim gives him the Unconditional Self-acceptance exercise to carry out for the following three months. He is given the task of challenging his rating, whether high or low, and to embrace instead the rules of the club. Martin agrees to try out these concepts. They also discuss the myth of self-esteem and how important it is to banish the concept for good.

Dr Jim is now ready to teach Martin some simple techniques to deal with his social interactional anxiety. He explains that social anxiety is all about our 'perceptions versus reality'. We believe, for example, that people can see the physical signs of anxiety. The reality, of course, is that these are quite difficult to detect. They also discuss the reality that 'people are self-obsessed' and rarely see or are interested in whether we are anxious or not. Often, they barely know we are in the room.

Dr Jim gives Martin some exercises to put these concepts into practice. The first is the Anxiety Inspector Exercise where he must find the anxious people in a social situation and report back on how he gets on. The other two are embarrassment exercises to trigger the emotion in 'safe' situations. These exercises (detailed in *Emotional Resilience*) are aimed at encouraging Martin to see what happens in social situations in real life versus his false misperceptions.

The real fun starts when they began to discuss the fourth exercise, namely the Conversation Exercise. Martin is forced to admit that part of his difficulties in relation to conversation lie in his belief that he is surrounded by 'boring' people on social situations and that he is only interested in talking about subjects interesting to himself.

Dr Jim then challenges this view.

'What subject do people like to talk about?' he asks.

Martin is forced to admit that most people, including himself, love to talk about themselves.

'But do you believe that constantly talking about yourself has assisted you to become a better conversationalist?' Dr Jim enquires.

Martin agrees that it had not been working so well 'to date'.

Dr Jim then lays out the exercise where, for the following few months, Martin would agree to focus completely on the person he was speaking to. Asking question after question about subjects they were aware the person was interested in and showing interest in their replies.

Martin is aghast that he would have to remove himself from the conversation.

'Is that not going to be so boring for me?' he asks.

Dr Jim then gives him a choice.

'Do you want to eliminate your social anxiety,' he asks, 'and accept the short-term discomfort of making other people comfortable while chatting socially to you?'

Martin agrees to try out this exercise constantly for the following three months.

This leads on to frank discussion on his final irrational belief or demand 'that he should not have to suffer discomfort' and 'that the world should change to suit him'.

'Is this rational or irrational?' Dr Jim enquires.

With reluctance, Martin agrees that is probably irrational. This leads to a challenging conversation about the world of 'low frustration tolerance' described by Dr Jim as 'seeking long-term gain but demanding that one should not have short-term pain'. So, the situation must change, not him.

Martin is forced to admit that this has been his '*modus operandi*' for many years and it had made him increasingly intolerant of himself and others. Dr Jim lays out some exercises, including the coin exercise, to assist him to deal with this irrational belief.

The next three months turn out to one of the busiest and most challenging periods of Martin's life to date. The various exercises transform his social anxiety and he is now increasingly comfortable in social situations and indeed with himself. He no longer puts so much pressure on himself to be the best at everything and accepts that he cannot rate or be rated as a human being. He is increasingly accepting that the world won't change to suit him. Most importantly, by a judicious use of the conversation exercise, he has met up with Barbara, who was impressed at how interested he was in her. She described him to her friends as so 'interesting'.

CONCLUSION

I had three main objectives in writing this book. The first was to put the myth of self-esteem under the microscope and comprehensively expose it for the delusion that I believe it to be. I hope that you will now agree or at least might question whether this concept is helping or (as I believe) damaging our mental health and well-being.

There may be some who believe that I as a health professional should not be challenging self-esteem. Hopefully most of you will be swayed by the evidence I have presented.

For self-esteem is damaging us individually and as a society. It is preventing us from becoming the wonderful, unique individuals that each one of us is. It is leading to a host of unhelpful initiatives and to a level of passivity in relation to taking responsibility for our skills and behaviour. It is, in my opinion, adding to rather than reducing the risks of anxiety, depression, eating disorders, even self-harm. If we believe as individuals that our 'worth' as a human being can be measured or valued, then trouble beckons. It is also preventing us from taking responsibility for our behaviour, a more challenging scenario.

There is also a darker side to self-esteem, which we have explored. We also examined the world of self- and other-rating and discussed how unhealthy and flawed it too can be.

Conclusion

My second task was to bring the work and words of Ellis back to the table, to encourage us to begin a revolution to challenge and replace the flawed worlds of self-esteem and self-rating with the concept of unconditional self-acceptance. This revolution involves us learning how to accept and love ourselves for the special, unique individuals we are. It will allow us to be more compassionate and respectful of ourselves, those we love and indeed all we meet on this crazy journey through life.

To accept ourselves without any conditions. To be content with oneself as a human being, just for being a member of humanity. And yet, most importantly, to take responsibility for all the actions we take in life. This is the revolutionary message that I wish you to take away from this book. Spread this message especially to your children, but also to the whole of society. Never has the world needed such a powerful message of love, freedom and hope as it struggles with the consequences which occur when powerful, ego-hungry leaders set the agenda. Where large multinational companies are encouraging us down the road of treating human beings as commodities. Where such powerful entities suggest that we can be rated and measured as human beings but based on completely superficial trappings, which they of course are happy to supply, at a cost!

Where powerful social media and technological companies are controlling the flow of information into our smartphones and other devices. All designed to make us rate, measure, judge and above all consume. Self-esteem and self-rating are food and drink to many of these vested interests which now deceptively control us, whether we like it or not. There are billions to be made from convincing us that we need to magically boost our self-esteem!

There is a danger that we are being subsumed into a quagmire of superficiality, where it is our looks, appearances and social-media profiles that matter, not who we are as human beings, or the hard-won achievements of real heroes. Where the lowest common denominator is often the 'measurement'. Where sensationalism and being famous for being famous is now seen as the norm. Where truth itself is often the victim.

Maybe it is time for us as a society to assess whether the messages we are currently passing on to our children are helping or damaging their future mental health. Perhaps it is time for unconditional self-acceptance rather than self-esteem the myth to become the path we encourage them to travel, if we genuinely wish them to become mature citizens of our brave new world.

My final task was to assist you in nurturing and growing your mental health by learning how to banish concepts such as self-esteem, self-worth and personal self-rating and replace them with unconditional self-acceptance. I hope that you stayed with me on this journey and saw yourself in many of the stories detailed in the latter part of the book. Learning how to love and accept yourself for being the unique human person you, the reader, are, and yet accepting full responsibility for your behaviour and skills. This is the real secret to your emotional resilience and positive mental health and well-being.

Between us, you and I can achieve the twin objectives of learning to be at ease with ourselves and the world whilst making the world we live in a better place for our children and generations to come.

BIBLIOGRAPHY

Introduction

Barry, H. P. (2017). *Emotional Resilience: How to safeguard your mental health.* Orion Spring.

Singai, J. (1917). 'How the Self-Esteem Craze Took Over America and why the hype was irresistible', *The Cut, New York Magazine.*

World Health Organization (2013). 'What is mental health?' (www.who.int/features/qa/62/en).

Part One: The Myth of Self-esteem

1. The Myth of Self-esteem

Amianto, F., Northoff, G., Abbate Daga, G., Fassino, S. and Tasca, G. A. (2016). 'Is Anorexia Nervosa a Disorder of the Self? A Psychological Approach', *Frontiers in Psychology*, 7, 849.

Barbarich-Marsteller, N. C., Foltin R. W. and Walsh, B. T. (2011). 'Does Anorexia Nervosa Resemble an Addiction?', *Current drug abuse reviews.* 4(3):197–200.

Barry, H.P. (2017). *Emotional Resilience: How to safeguard your mental health.* Orion Spring.

Baumeister, R. J., Campbell, J. D., Krueger, J. I. and Vohs, K. D. (2003). 'Does High Self-esteem cause better performance, interpersonal success, happiness or healthier lifestyles?', *Psychological Science in the Public Interest* 4:1.

Baumeister, R. J., Campbell, J. D., Krueger, J. I. and Vohs, K. D. (2005). 'Exploding the Self-Esteem Myth', *Scientific American*, 292, 84–91.

Chemers, M. M., Watson, C. B. and May, S. T. (2000). 'Dispositional affect and leadership effectiveness: A comparison of self-esteem, optimism, and efficacy', *Personality and Social Psychology Bulletin*, 26(3), 267–7.

Crocker, J., Luhtanen, R. K., Cooper, M. L. and Bouvrette, A. (2003). 'Contingencies of Self-Worth in College Students: Theory and Measurement', *Journal of Personality and Social Psychology*, 85(5), 894–908.

Crocker, J. and Park L. E. (2004). 'The Costly Pursuit of Self-Esteem', *Psychological Bulletin*. 130(3):392–414.

Crocker, J., Lee, S. J., & Park, L. E. (2004). 'The pursuit of self-esteem: Implications for good and evil', *The Social Psychology of Good and Evil*, 271–302. New York: Guilford Press.

Crocker J. and Carnevale J. (2013). 'Letting go of self-esteem', *Scientific America Mind*, 24 (4), 27–33.

Diagnostic and Statistical Manual of Mental Disorders (*DSM–5*).

Emler, N. (2001). 'The costs and causes of low self-esteem', Layerthorpe for the Joseph Rowntree Foundation.

Graham, D. Y (2014). 'History of *Helicobacter pylori*, duodenal ulcer, gastric ulcer and gastric cancer', *World Journal of Gastroenterology*, 20 (18): 5191–204.

Harrison, J. E., Barry, H., Baune, B. T., Best, M. W., Bowie, C. R., Cha, D. S., Culpepper, L., Fossati P., Greer, T. L., Harmer, C.,

Klag, E., Lam, R. W., Rodrigo, Y. L., Mansur, R. M., Wittchen H. U. and McIntyre, R. S. (2018). 'Stability, reliability, and validity of the THINC- It screening tool for cognitive impairment in depression: A psychometric exploration in healthy volunteers, *International Journal of Methods in Psychiatric Research*. 27: 3.

Hongfei, D., King, R .B. & Peilian, C. (2017). 'Self-esteem and subjective well-being revisited: The roles of personal, relational, and collective self-esteem', *PLOS ONE*.

International Statistical Classification of Diseases and Related Health Problems (1CD – 10).

James, W. (1983). *The Principles of Psychology*. Cambridge, MA: Harvard University Press. (Original work published 1890).

Kawamichi, H., Sugawara, Y. H. *et al*. (2018). 'Neural correlates underlying change in state self-esteem'. *Sci Rep*, 8 (1):1798.

Libby, P. (2008). 'Atherosclerosis: The New View', *Scientific American* (www.scientificamerican.com/article/ atherosclerosis-the-new-view).

Manna, G., Falgares, G., Ingoglia, S., Como, R. S., and De Santis, S. (2016) 'The Relationship between Self-Esteem, Depression and Anxiety: Comparing Vulnerability and Scar Model in the Italian Context', *Mediterranean Journal of Clinical Psychology* 4:3.

Mruk, C. (2010). 'Self Esteem'. In W. E. Craighead and C. B. Nemeroff (eds), *The Corsini Encyclopedia of Psychology and Behavioral Science (4th ed.). Hoboken, NJ: Wiley* OxfordDictionaries.com

Piotrowski, A. *et al*. (2008). 'Phenotypically Concordant and Discordant Monozygotic Twins Display Different DNA Copy-Number-Variation Profiles', *The American Journal of Human Genetics*, 82, 763–71.

Pozin, I. (2014). '16 Leadership Quotes to Inspire You to Greatness'. *Forbes Magazine* (www.forbes.com/sites/ilyapozin/2014/04/10/16-leadership-quotes-to-inspire-you-to-greatness).

Riva G. (2016). 'Neurobiology of Anorexia Nervosa: Serotonin Dysfunctions Link Self-Starvation with Body Image Disturbances through an Impaired Body Memory', *Frontiers in Human Neuroscience* 10:600.

Rodewalt, F. and Tragakis, M. W. (2003). 'Self-Esteem and Self-Regulation: Toward Optimal Studies of Self-Esteem', *Psychological Inquiry, 14,* 66–70.

Rosenberg, M. (1965). *Society and the Adolescent Self-Image.* Princeton, NJ: Princeton University Press.

The Key for School Leaders. (2018). 'Boosting Pupil's Self-esteem'. (www.schoolleaders.thekeysupport.com/pupils-and-parents/pupil-health-and-wellbeing/pupil-wellbeing/boosting-children2019s-self-esteem).

Vohs, K. D., Bardone, A. M., Joiner, T. E., Jr, Abramson, L. Y., & Heatherton, T. F. (1999). 'Perfectionism, perceived weight status, and self-esteem interact to predict bulimic symptoms: A model of bulimic symptom development', *Journal of Abnormal Psychology,* 108, 695–700.

Vohs, K. D., Voelz, Z. R., Pettit, J. W., Bardone, A. M., Katz, J., Abramson, L. Y., Heatherton, T. F., & Joiner, T. E., Jr (2001). 'Perfectionism, body dissatisfaction, and self-esteem: An interactive model of bulimic symptom development', *Journal of Social and Clinical Psychology,* 20, 476–96.

2. Self-acceptance

Barry, H. P. (2017). *Emotional Resilience: How to safeguard your mental health.* Orion Spring.

Ellis, A. (1962). *Reason and Emotion in Psychotherapy.* Lyle Stuart, New York.

Ellis, A. (1996), *Better, Deeper and More Enduring Brief Therapy: The Rational Emotive Therapy Approach.* Brunner/Mazel Inc., New York.

James, W. (1983). *The Principles of Psychology.* Cambridge, MA: Harvard University Press. (Original work published 1890).

3. The Dark Side of Self-esteem

Abbasi, I. S., Alghamdi N. G. (2015). 'The Prevalence, Predictors, Causes, Treatments, and Implications of Procrastination Behaviours in General, Academic, and Work Setting', *International Journal of Psychological Studies*, Vol. 7, No. 1.

Aiken, M. (2016). *The Cyber Effect: A pioneering cyberpsychologist explains how human behaviour changes online.* John Murray Press.

Amianto, F., Northoff, G., Daga, D. A., Fassino S. and Tasca, G. A. *(2016)* 'Is Anorexia Nervosa a Disorder of the Self? A Psychological Approach.' *Front. Psychol. 7:849.*

Aronia, S., and Smith, M. (2018). 'One in four students suffer from mental health problems', YouGov UK.

Barry, H., and Murphy, E. (2015). *Flagging the Screenager: Guiding your child through adolescence and young adulthood.* Liberties Press, Dublin.

Bonnette, R. (2014). 'Rethinking Technology's Impact on Empathy', Loyola University Chicago, School of Law

Botou, A., and Marsellos, P.S. (2018). 'Teens' Perception about Social Networking Sites: Does Facebook Influence Teens' Self-Esteem?', *Psychology,* 9, 1453–74.

Brummelman, E., Thomaes, S., Nelemans, S., Castro, B., Overbeek, G., and Bushman, B. (2015). 'Origins of narcissism in children', *Proceedings of the National Academy of Sciences of the United States of America*. 112 (12), 3659–62.

Brummelman, E., Crocker and Bushman, B. (2016). 'The Praise Paradox: When and why praise backfires in children with low self-esteem', *Child Development Perspectives*. 10 (2), 111–115.

Doerig, N., Schlumpf, Y., Spinelli, S., Spati, J., Brakowski, B., Quednow *et al.* (2014). 'Neural representation and clinically relevant moderators of individualised self-criticism in healthy subjects', *Social Cognitive and Affective Neuroscience*, 9: 9, 1333–40.

Dooley, B., and Fitzgerald, A. (2012). 'My world survey', Headstrong – The National Centre for Youth Mental Health, Dublin and UCD School of Psychology, Dublin.

Hale, L. and Guan, S. (2015). 'Screen Time and Sleep among School-Aged Children and Adolescents: A Systematic Literature Review', *Sleep Medicine Reviews* Jun; 21: 50–58.

Horgan, A., Kelly P., Goodwin, J. and Behan L. (2018). 'Depressive Symptoms and Suicidal Ideation among Irish Undergraduate College Students', *Issues in Mental Health Nursing*'. 39(7): 575–84.

Hunt. E. (2017). 'Teenagers' sleep quality and mental health at risk over late-night mobile phone use', *Guardian*. (www.theguardian.com/lifeandstyle/2017/may/30/teenagers-sleep-quality-and-mental-health-at-risk-over-late-night-mobile-phone-use).

Joint Commissioning Panel for Mental Health (2011). (www.jcpmh.info/wp-content/uploads/10keymsgs-eatingdisorders.pdf).

Karwig, G., Chambers D. and Murphy, F. (2015). 'Reaching Out in College: Help-Seeking at Third Level in Ireland', *Reach Out Ireland*. (https://ie.reachout.com/wp-content/uploads/2015/11/research-report-final-lo-res.pdf).

Konrath, S.H., O'Brien, E.H. and Hsing C. (2011). 'Changes in Dispositional Empathy in American College Students Over Time: A Meta-Analysis', *Personality and Social Psychology Review*. Vol 15, issue 2.

Levenson, J. C., Shensa A., Sidani J.E., Colditz, J.B. and Primack B.A. (2016). 'The Association between Social Media Use and Sleep Disturbance among Young Adults', *Preventive Medicine*. 85: 36–41.

McGrath, M. (2016). 'Selfie society: Are the Kardashians ruining womanhood?', *Independent.ie*. (www.independent.ie/style/voices/selfie-society-are-the-kardashians-ruining-womanhood-35201655.html).

McLafferty, M., Lapsley, C. R., Ennis, E., Armour, C., Murphy, S. *et al.* (2017). 'Mental health, behavioural problems and treatment seeking among students commencing university in Northern Ireland', *PLOS ONE*. 12(12).

McMahon, E. M., Keeley, H., Cannon, M., Arensman, Perry, I. J., Clarke, M., Chambers, D. and Corcoran, P. (2014). 'The iceberg of suicide and self-harm in Irish adolescents: a population-based study', *Social Psychiatry Psychiatry Epidemiology*.

McMahon, E. M., O'Regan, G., Corcoran, P., Arensman, E., Cannon, M., Williamson, E. and Keeley, H. (2017). *Young Lives in Ireland: a school-based study of mental health and suicide prevention*. Cork: National Suicide Research Foundation.

Marsh. S. (2017). 'Number of university dropouts due to mental health problems trebles', *Guardian*. (www.theguardian.com/

society/2017/may/23/number-university-dropouts-due-to-mental-health-problems-trebles).

Odgers, C. (2018). 'Smartphones are bad for some teens, not all. Young people who are already struggling offline might experience greater negative effects of life online. *Nature.* 554: 432–4.

Ofcom (2017). 'Children and Parents: Media Use and Attitudes Report'.

Pasquinelli, E. (2018). 'Are Digital Devices Altering Our Brains? Some say our gadgets and computers can help improve intelligence. Others say they make us stupid and violent. Which is it?', *Scientific American Mind.* (www.scientificamerican.com/article/are-digital-devices-altering-our-brains).

Przybylski, A. K. and Weinstein, N. (2017). 'A Large-Scale Test of the Goldilocks Hypothesis Quantifying the Relations Between Digital-Screen Use and the Mental Well-Being of Adolescents', *N. Psychol. Sci. 28*, 204–15.

Reilly, E. E., Stey, P. and Lapsley, D. K. (2016). 'A new look at the links between perceived parenting, socially-prescribed perfectionism, and disordered eating', *Personality and Individual Differences.* 88: 17–20.

Reilly, K. (2018). 'Record numbers of college students are seeking treatment for depression and anxiety – but schools can't keep up', *Time* magazine. (www.time.com/5190291/anxiety-depression-college-university-students).

Rock, P. L., Roiser, J. P., Riedel, W. J. and Blackwell, A. D. (2013). 'Cognitive impairment in depression: a systematic review and meta-analysis', *Psychol Med,* 1–12.

Royal Society for Public Health/Young Health Movement (2017) – *Status of Mind.*

Bibliography

Rudgard, O. (2018). 'Universities have a suicide problem as students taking their own lives, overtakes general population', *The Telegraph*. (www.telegraph.co.uk/news/2018/04/12/universities-have-suicide-problem-students-taking-lives-overtakes).

Rudgard, O. (2018) 'Why are Silicon Valley execs banning their kids from using social media?', *The Telegraph*. (www.telegraph.co.uk/family/parenting/silicon-valley-execs-invented-social-media-wont-let-kids-use).

Schrobsdorff, S. (2016). 'Teen depression and anxiety: why the kids are not alright'. *Time* magazine.

Smith, M. M., Sherry, S. B., Chen S., Saklofske, D. H., Mushquash, C., Flett, G. L. and Hewitt, P. L. (2017). 'The perniciousness of perfectionism: A meta-analytic review of the perfectionism–suicide relationship', *Journal Personality*. 00:1–20.

Solon, O. (2016). 'Smartphones Won't Make Your Kids Dumb – We Think. Are screens a sinister trap or magical portal for children as young as 18 months?', *Scientific American*. (www.scientificamerican.com/article/smartphones-won-t-make-your-kids-dumb-we-think).

Sweeting, H., Walker, L., MacLean, A., Patterson, C., Räisänen, U., Hunt, K. (2015). 'Prevalence of eating disorders in males: a review of rates reported in academic research and UK mass media'. *International Journal of Men's Health*. 14(2):10.

Szabo, M. K. (2015). 'The Relationship Between Body Image and Self-esteem', *European Psychiatry*: 30:(1) 1354.

Thistleton, K. (2018). 'Is it time we all unfollowed Kim Kardashian?' BBC Radio One. (www.bbc.co.uk/bbcthree/article/85f1f633-bfbb-4928-b487-72da9bd9b225).

Thompson, S. (2017). 'There is a tsunami of third-level students with mental health problems', *Irish Times*. (www.irishtimes.com/news/education/there-is-a-tsunami-of-third-level-students-with-mental-health-problems-1.2924516).

Part Two: Unconditional Self-acceptance

5. The Pathological Critic

Barry, H.P. (2017). *Emotional Resilience: How to safeguard your mental health*. Orion Spring.

Doerig, N., Schlumpf, Y., Spinelli, S., Spati, J., Brakowski, B., Quednow *et al.* (2014). 'Neural representation and clinically relevant moderators of individualised self-criticism in healthy subjects', *Social Cognitive and Affective Neuroscience*, 9: 9, 1333–40.

Hamilton, P. J., Farmer, M., Fogelman, P. and Gotlib, H. (2015). 'Depressive Rumination, the Default-Mode Network, and the Dark Matter of Clinical Neuroscience', *Biol Psychiatry*. 78(4): 224–30.

Nejad, A. B., Fossati, P. and Lemogne, C. (2013). 'Self-referential processing, rumination, and cortical midline structures in major depression', *Front Hum Neurosci*. 7:666.

Zhu, Xueling *et al.* (2017). 'Rumination and Default Mode Network Subsystems Connectivity in First-episode, Drug-Naive Young Patients with Major Depressive Disorder', *Scientific reports* 7: 43105.

6. Unconditional Self-acceptance

Barry, H.P. (2017). *Emotional Resilience: How to safeguard your mental health*. Orion Spring.

Bibliography

Ellis, A. (1962). *Reason and Emotion in Psychotherapy,* Lyle Stuart, New York.

Ellis, A. (1996). *Better, Deeper and More Enduring Brief Therapy: The Rational Emotive Therapy Approach.* Brunner/Mazel Inc., New York.

INDEX

ACKNOWLEDGEMENTS

I would like to start as always, by thanking my editorial team in Orion for all their wonderful assistance in publishing this book. I want to especially thank my editor Olivia Morris who has believed in the Flag series from the beginning and who has been so supportive, guiding me patiently along the right path in relation to this book. I am also indebted to Amanda Harris, publisher at Seven Dials and Orion Spring for her major input into the final production of *Self-Acceptance*. I am also indebted as always to desk editor Ru Merritt for her assistance and patience in bringing it all together, and to my publicity managers Elizabeth Allen in the UK and Elaine Egan from Hachette Ireland and Amy Davies, for their assistance in the PR and social media marketing areas.

I also owe a huge debt of gratitude to Vanessa Fox O'Loughlin and Dominic Perrim, my two agents who have made this project possible.

I would like to especially thank my dear friend and colleague Dr Muiris Houston of the *Irish Times*, for taking the time to review the text, and for his friendship and support. His reports in the excellent Health Plus supplement are respected by us all.

I send the warmest of thanks to my good friend Cathy Kelly (bestselling author and UNICEF ambassador) for her constant kindness and support throughout the years. I am also indebted to my good friend and national treasure, Sr Stan, founder of Focus Ireland and The Sanctuary, who embodies what this book is about.

I am, as always, indebted to my friend and colleague Enda Murphy for his invaluable assistance. A brilliant CBT therapist and former ICGP tutor, who has taught me much of what I know; I am deeply grateful for his support and insightful comments. We share a joint vision of where mental health should be moving towards. We both value our national radio slot with the Sean O'Rourke show very highly, and I would like to take this opportunity to thank Sean (a true gentleman of Irish media) and his wonderful team, particularly Cora Ennis and series producer Tara Campbell, for allowing us the opportunity to highlight key areas of mental health. A special thanks to Hannah Parkes, Alistair Mc Connell, Geraldine Collins, Mary O' Hagan amongst many others for their constant support over the years.

I am deeply indebted to my colleague, Catherine Harmer, Professor of Cognitive Neuroscience at Oxford, for her support and for taking time out of her busy schedule to review this work. I would like to thank Julia O' Hegarty Consultant Senior Content Editor of the *Financial Times* and organiser of the St John Ambulance Mental Health Summit in London 2018, who was not only kind enough to ask me to address the meeting but who also took the time to review and support this book. Thank you, Julia. I would also like to thank Bruce Daisley, Vice-President for Twitter Europe and bestselling author of the *Sunday Times* No.1 bestseller *The Joy of Work* for kindly agreeing to review the script.

Special thanks as always to friend and colleague Professor Patricia Casey of University College Dublin, who has been so supportive over the years and for once again reviewing this book.

I am also extremely grateful to friend and colleague Professor Cathal Kelly, Registrar and CEO of RCSI, who took time out of his busy schedule to review the book and thanks also to his lovely wife Ruth. I was also delighted that Professor Ian Robertson, Professor Psychology Trinity College Dublin, and eminent psychologist Fiona Doherty both agreed to review the script. I am extremely grateful to you both.

I was also especially honoured that friend and colleague Senator Joan Freeman, Chairperson of the Oireachtas Joint Committee on the Future of Mental Health and who has done so much for suicide prevention in Ireland and USA, took time out to review the book, too.

I am also so appreciative to my international colleagues: Professor Ray Lam at the University of British Columbia, Canada; Bernhard Baune, Professor of Psychiatry at the University of Adelaide, Australia; and Professor Larry Culpepper, at Boston University, USA – all of whom have been so supportive and have taken the time to review this book.

I must send a special thanks to my Club Foursomes-winning partner and good friend Dan Hughes, a truly talented golfer who has (along with my family) kept me sane during the writing of this book.

I say a special thanks to my sons Daniel and Joseph (and his wife Sue and my beautiful granddaughter Saoirse) and to my daughter Lara (and her husband Hans and my two much loved grandsons Ciaran and Sean) for all their love and support and for keeping me well grounded!

As always, I reserve my biggest 'thank you' to my wife Brenda, whose love, friendship, support, encouragement, and particularly patience has made this book and indeed the whole series possible. You will always have my back as I have yours. You are my light in the darkness, and truly my soulmate. 'Mo ghra, mo chroi' (my love, my heart).

ABOUT THE AUTHOR

Dr Harry Barry is a highly respected Irish author and medic, with over three decades of experience as a GP. With a keen interest in the area of mental health and suicide prevention, Dr Barry is the author of numerous books addressing various aspects of mental health including anxiety, depression, toxic stress and emotional resilience.

A practical guide teaching you how to best tackle life's challenges.

'Another masterpiece from a cutting-edge expert'
Dr Muiris Houston,
The Irish Times

EMOTIONAL
RESILIENCE

How to safeguard your
mental health

THE BRAND NEW BOOK FROM
INTERNATIONAL BESTSELLING AUTHOR

DR HARRY BARRY